MW01034895

The Beautiful Itself Is Reality Itself Is Truth Itself Is

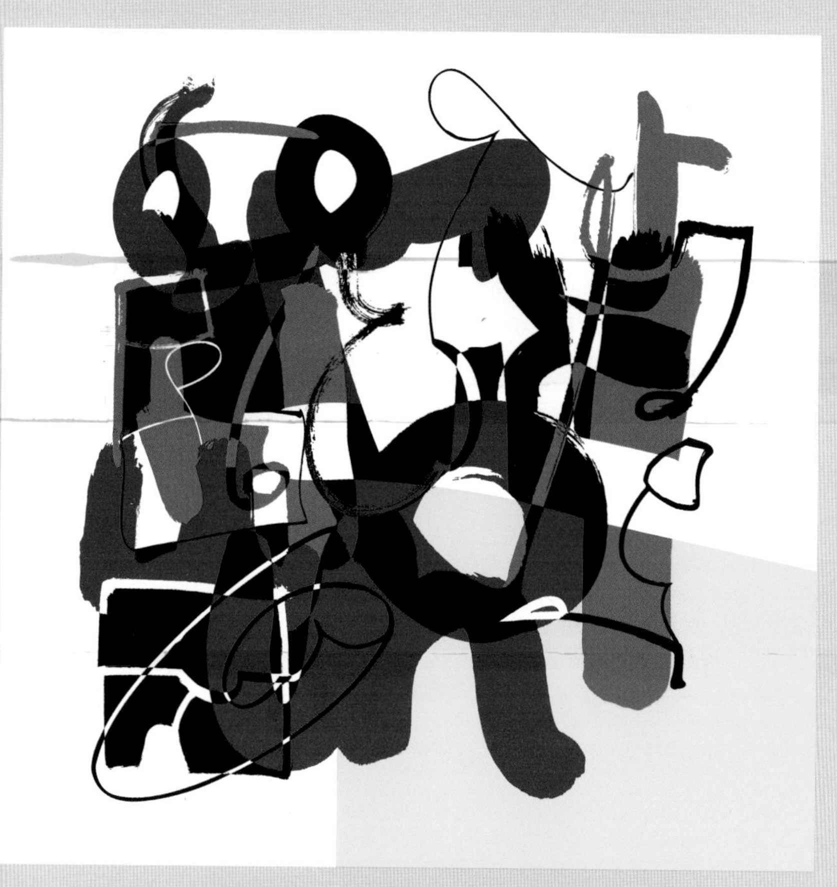

Childish Conrad and The Evil Thumb-Tailor,
or, The Boogeyman Always Bobs Both
(It Is Your Fear What Takes The Life Out Of You,
Because The Mind Always Deceives The Body), 208,
from *The Struwwelpeter Suite (The ego-"I" and The Straightener):*
Contemplating The Mind/Body Problem
and The Bodily Illusion Of Being a Separate "self",
Part Six, 2008

TRANSCENDENTAL REALISM

The Image-Art of egoless Coincidence With Reality Itself

Adi Da Samraj

THE DAWN HORSE PRESS
MIDDLETOWN, CALIFORNIA

Second edition, August 2010
The second edition of *Transcendental Realism* contains all the essays that Adi Da Samraj wrote for this book (between 2006 and 2008)—including the essays from the first edition (2007), the essays originally published in the books *Aesthetic Ecstasy* (2007) and *Perfect Abstraction* (2008), and the essays written by Adi Da Samraj after those three publications.

Produced by the Dawn Horse Press.

International Standard Book Number: 978-1-57097-285-0
Library of Congress Catalog Card Number: 2010929020

The image on the first page of *Transcendental Realism* is a "circular motto" composed and handwritten by Adi Da Samraj, and placed within an arrangement of square, circle, and triangle, the three geometric forms that are fundamental structural elements in much of his artwork.

CONTENTS

Transcendental Realism

by Adi Da Samraj

INTRODUCTION

by Erik van Erp, PhD

"Art then is a becoming and happening of truth."

—Martin Heidegger
"The Origin of the Work of Art"

Art speaks for itself, in silence. Yet, some words can be spoken to assist its reception. In the text you have before you, *Transcendental Realism*, the artist, Adi Da Samraj, speaks of his art, his purposes, and the unique artistic discipline by which those purposes are realized. This is an unusual text. You will find that it does not conform easily to familiar categories of "art speak". It will not fit in comfortably and unobtrusively in the mental planes of discourse that surround modern art. It resists quick and easy digestion, even by those of sophisticated intellect. Like Adi Da's art itself, this text is a confrontation, and is deeply at odds with the trends of post-modernism. It requires—and deserves—attentive reading.

Adi Da crafts his writings with the same serious intent and meticulous discipline with which he makes his images. More than a verbal explanation of what his art is "really" all about, this body of words, much like Adi Da's art itself, is a "transformational environment". If you have seen Adi Da's art, and wonder what or who it was that moved you, a careful consideration of this text will serve to integrate the immediacy of the aesthetic experience into a transformed understanding—of Adi Da's art, of art altogether, and of the most profound dimensions of human experience.

The text of *Transcendental Realism* is a speaking that accompanies the art. It requires, first of all, a right viewing of the art. The words of this artist must be heard in the same open space in which his art exists. An introduction like this runs the risk of performing the anti-miracle of turning wine into water. Schopenhauer once remarked that scholars who write commentary on great philosophy are filtering great intelligence through a small mind, which is like trying to fit the ocean in a thimble. Adi Da's text is poetic, yet precise; profoundly logical, yet full of paradox. And, while requiring thoughtful study, its meanings do not reside, exactly, at the level of thought.

On the first page of the book is printed a circular word-image, "Reality Itself Is Truth Itself Is The Beautiful Itself Is . . . ". This, at once, defines the circle of essential meaning in which the text moves. It is a circle that encompasses Plato, the Upanishads, and the alchemical experiments of Gertrude Stein. It is a circle in which antiquity meets modernism—a circle that freely embraces all serious achievements of human civilization and culture. There is no irony here, no post-modern tongue-in-cheek. In *Transcendental Realism*, Adi Da announces his serious intent to renew the "modernist" program, and he is not going to settle for less than the traditionally required measure of art as Reality, Truth, The Beautiful, realized as an indivisible unity.

The text itself is a perfect circle, an integrated whole that is hard to break into "chewable" pieces without removing its essential force. It proceeds from the universal to the particular—without, in fact, ever leaving the universal. Adi Da always returns the reader to the unity of Being, no matter what the topic under consideration. This "circularity" (or indivisible unity) that underlies the text is responsible for the astounding depth of its beginning. The first essay of the book presents a tower of meaning on a single page. Through the universality and reiterations of its statement, it connects to the circular poem on the first page. But here the circle is manifested in the guise of logic. The language is precise, mathematical, without redundancy. But the logic guides us into an abyss of meaning, where the mind loses its foothold. As best as language can support it, Adi Da states here how the measure of art (and all culture) is grounded in reality. In Adi Da's understanding, there is nothing arbitrary about true culture. True culture is grounded in reality. Virtue is grounded in reality. Art, and its rightful purpose, is grounded in reality. And to be grounded in reality, the book, at its very "beginning", must call its own language into being, and provide its own context.

To reach his end, and to elaborate his beginning, Adi Da repeatedly utilizes a specific set of ordinary words. While starting out with their familiar meanings, their repeated use in gradually widening circles pushes their meanings in new and unheard-of directions. This linguistic strategy is akin to that of the philosopher Martin Heidegger. There is, in fact, a certain affinity between this text and Heidegger's writings. To be sure, there is no "influence" of Heidegger's thinking here, no direct reference. The affinity is more essential. Heidegger's sole concern was to re-insert the question of the meaning of Being into the heart of philosophy. He realized that the failure of his first attempts in this direction was deeply related to the very character and project of Western metaphysics. Metaphysics proceeds from "beings" to Being, by questioning "beings" as to their mode of being, thus hoping to arrive at the truth of Being Itself. Instead, Heidegger thought, if we are to attempt to speak of Being Itself, our very speaking must originate <u>from</u> Being, instead of merely moving <u>toward</u> it. This required a profound historical leap. Whether Heidegger's own attempts in this direction were successful is open to debate. But one is reminded of the struggle of this great philosopher when one reads that Adi Da creates his art as "a Self-Portrait of Reality Itself", and regards his artistic discipline as a means to enable "the Direct (and Intrinsically egoless) Self-Presentation of Reality Itself". What Adi Da presents us with, it seems, is a sign of that historical "leap" and new beginning that Heidegger, in his philosophical intuitions, knew in his time.

While the aim of *Transcendental Realism* is not primarily to elaborate his radical "philosophy" on the nature of Reality, Adi Da's artistic purposes, his consideration of the nature of his own art (and even all art), and his description of his unique manner of working are all grounded and elaborated in the context of this fundamental understanding. Adi Da has, of necessity, developed his own unique language to do his speaking, because of the radical nature of what is being said. Adi Da's language enables him to express transcendental purposes without getting trapped in metaphysics, and its movement to "elsewhere". It is also through this language that Adi Da redefines, in radical terms, some of the basic categories of modern art—specifically, "representational art", "objective art", and "subjective art". These terms are redefined, re-evaluated, and even "measured" against Adi Da's unique understanding of Reality and its inherent demands.

One of the fundamental notions in this remarkable text is what Adi Da calls "transcending 'point of view'". The consideration of "point of view"—sometimes under the name of "perspective"—is, of course, a familiar theme in art criticism, and plays a pivotal role in discourse on modernism. Adi Da's treatment of the notion deliberately links up with that artistic tradition. But the notion of "point of view" has many connotations, and its meaning could equally well be considered in the context of modern physics or neuroscience. Adi Da's use of the term freely references all such contexts of meaning. But those familiar references serve as the starting point for the communication of an essentially new understanding. In direct contrast to the common understanding of the term, Adi Da holds that "point of view" is not inherent to perception itself! One could say that there can be "viewing" without "point of view". Thus, Adi Da states that "point of view" is not necessary—and, indeed, is entirely fictitious. Not just what is seen "from" a "point of view" is illusory (or incomplete, or in whatever way presumed to be distorted), but the very presumption that the perceiver is located at a "point" in space-time (perhaps somewhere inside the brain), always "stepped back" from what is being viewed, is itself the root-illusion.

One pole, or aspect, of "point of view" is the false presumption that there is some kind of permanent center of attention—an "ego", or "self", or "subject"—at the root, or somewhere "inside", of experience. On the "other side" of attention, "objects" are co-constructed with the "ego". Once "point of view" is assumed, there seems to be some field that exists independently and "outside" of attention, as the world of "things" (or "objects") onto which attention casts its eye. But Adi Da maintains that "there are no 'objects' in Reality Itself". This does not mean to say that reality exists as some kind of subjective dream. Rather, both the "subjective self" and its "world of objects"—as separate and independent "somethings"—are illusory, or without real being.

"Reality Itself", then, is expressly not the Kantian *Ding an sich*, or "thing itself". It is not the "objective world" of ordinary "realism". But neither is it the merely "subjective" realm of "idealism". It is, most simply, that which is the case, as opposed to that which is presumed to be the case. And in "It" there exists no "point of view". Reality Itself is not knowable from any defined "point of view". However, in every instant in which "point of view" is transcended—that is, in every moment in which one forgets to actively "create" one's experience in the mold of the ego-and-its-objects—Reality Itself is Self-Apprehended as Truth Itself, and as The Beautiful Itself, in what Adi Da calls "egoless Coincidence with Reality Itself". It is in that egoless state that Adi Da makes his images, and it is that same state into which the viewer is drawn by right participation in his art.

Against this background, the specifics of Adi Da's artistic discipline and his manner of creating images can be understood and appreciated. For example, Adi Da's description of the process of abstraction in relation to the always present meaning-context of his art, and his rejection of the alternatives of "subjective" self-expression versus "objective" representation, are clarified and grounded in that universal consideration.

Conversely, the essays in which Adi Da elaborates the principles and details of his artistic process add further clarity to his consideration of Reality, by showing, very concretely and specifically, how Reality Itself is set to work in the spontaneous discipline of his image-making, and how no "point of view" needs to enter the picture.

The various layers of meaning of the text are thus inseparable. Ultimately, what Adi Da communicates here is not something that is meant to be grasped by mental effort alone. Real "understanding" would entail the transcending of "point of view" in the reader. It is exactly to serve that process that Adi Da makes his art. "Art is the setting-into-work of truth", says Heidegger. In the sensuous sphere of mere perception, in direct participation in the "space" of Adi Da's images, the fullest meaning of the text is tacitly communicated.

So enjoy and be illuminated by these words and images. Let the "geometry" of Adi Da's text fold itself into the tissues of your thought—its straight lines of analytic clarity, the circular and centerless unity of its origin and purpose, and the sharp angles it makes with the plane of the familiar. Through the rapture of aesthetic pleasure, and the cracks of inevitable discomfort, Adi Da reveals his secrets and opens up the groundless ground of Being. ■

Adi Da Samraj

The Master of the Transformational Art of Transcendental Realism

As he relates in his autobiography, *The Knee of Listening*, the entire life of Adi Da Samraj (1939–2008) was characterized by a unique transcendental state of spiritual illumination. Adi Da described his early years as being focused in two fundamental activities: (1) investigating what is required for human beings to realize the true nature of reality, and (2) achieving the ability to communicate the true nature of reality through artistic means, both visual and literary.

Adi Da Samraj graduated from Columbia University in 1961, with a BA in philosophy (including much concentration in both art and literature), and from Stanford University in 1966, with an MA in English literature. His master's thesis, a study of core issues in modernism, focused on the literary experiments of Gertrude Stein and on the modernist painters of the same period. This study of modernist literature and painting was an early sign of Adi Da's abiding interest in the modernist effort to break beyond the bounds of the perspectival "point of view" and to investigate the realities of perception and conscious awareness. His own artistic and literary works were intended to complete the modernist impulse, by going beyond "point of view" altogether and thereby conveying the core realities of conscious existence.

In 1972, Adi Da Samraj began to offer his transcendental spiritual way and his "reality-teaching" to the world, creating a vast repository of wisdom, in living dialogue with those who approached him as devotees. His literary, spiritual, philosophical, and practical writings consist of over seventy-five published books—many internationally acclaimed. In the early 1970s, Alan Watts, writer of numerous books on religion and philosophy, acknowledged Adi Da Samraj as "a rare being", adding, "It is obvious, from all sorts of subtle details, that he knows what IT's all about." In the late 1990s, poet Robert Lax said of Adi Da's radically experimental novel, *The Mummery Book*, "Living and working as a writer for many decades, I have not encountered a book like this, that mysteriously and unselfconsciously conveys so much of the unspeakable reality."

Adi Da Samraj began serious work in the photographic medium in the early 1960s. From the mid-60s to the mid-90s, he produced works in a variety of two-dimensional and three-dimensional media—works characterized by freedom, spontaneity, humor, and the impulse to stretch the bounds of the given medium. Between 1998 and early 2004, he concentrated in camera-based imagery (both photographic and videographic), creating a large and highly complex body of work. His work in the photographic medium moved from black-and-white to highly saturated color, featuring multiple exposures composed in-camera. His primary bodies of work from this period use the figurative form and other archetypes to address the deepest issues of human existence, and use multiple exposure in particular as a powerful means to investigate "point of view" and the process of transcending it.

In early 2006, Adi Da Samraj initiated a new phase in his artistic work, by beginning to work entirely in the digital medium. This new medium afforded him a virtually unlimited degree of complexity. In his digitally-based work, it was Adi Da's intention to work with color and shape in a radical manner—a manner that directly reflects both the root-structure (and the "transcendental reality-condition") of physical reality and (coincidently) the root-manner in which the brain processes the perception of physical reality.

Adi Da Samraj often included photographic and/or hand-drawn elements within the structures of his otherwise digitally-constructed images. In much of this work, there is only the most abstract evidence of the photographic or otherwise rendered "sketches" of his subjects. Nevertheless, as a fundamental principle of his art, Adi Da Samraj assumed a discipline of maintaining a "response to the subject", by making use of photographs (or other forms of imagery) of the subject he was contemplating.

In November 2007, Adi Da Samraj reached what he described as the "final resolution" of his entire artistic process. This turning point enabled him to create non-representational art by using a unique method he named "Orphic Font"—a method of generating abstract forms by making "collages of pictographs". Adi Da felt this work to be the culmination of his artistic oeuvre and philosophy, the fully realized expression of "transcendental realism".

Adi Da's works have been fabricated in many media, including monumentally-scaled paint on aluminum, large-scale pigmented inks on canvas, photographic and videographic works, sculptural light-boxes, plasma-screen installations, and multi-screen projected performance events.

Adi Da Samraj's work has been exhibited in galleries and museums throughout the United States and Europe. He was featured as an official solo collateral artist at the 2007 Venice Biennale. He was also invited by the City of Florence to be the first contemporary artist to exhibit his work in the renowned Cenacolo di Ognissanti.

Adi Da stated that his intention as an artist was to create images that enable the viewer to participate in the "vast unpatterned Joy" that is the ultimate nature of existence. ■

TRANSCENDENTAL REALISM

by

Adi Da Samraj

I.

The Only Subject of All Art

The "self"-responsive "self"-reflecting (and possible "self"-responsive "self"-representation) of the human "self"—including its body, its relations (both "subjective" and "objective"), its conditions, its environment (or world, or universe), its history (or auto-narrative of experience and "self"-development), and, ultimately, its own Source-Reality (or Inherently Perfect Self-Condition)—and the self-organizing of the "self"-understanding of the human "self" (and, ultimately, the Intrinsic, or Self-Evident, Self-Organizing of the Intrinsic Self-Apprehension of the Self-Condition of Reality Itself) is the necessary (and also traditional) "subject" of all art.

The principal "differences" between particular works of art are a matter of the humanly measurable degree or extent to which any and each particular work of art achieves (artistically) both exactness and universality relative to the comprehensive "event" of human "self"-apprehension—and, ultimately, the principal "differences" between particular works of art are a matter of the only tacitly measurable (and, otherwise, Inherently Immeasurable) degree or extent to which any and each particular work of art achieves authentic rightness and trueness relative to the aesthetic (and, altogether, Real) "event" of the Tacit Intrinsic Self-Apprehension of the Self-Condition of Reality Itself.

II.

Art and Chaos

The spoken-sung word is the source from which the art of music is taken (and which it duplicates, represents, extends, and abstracts).

The written-pictured word is the source from which the art of image is taken (and which it duplicates, represents, extends, and abstracts).

The spoken-sung-written-pictured word (and its word-mind altogether) is the source from which the art of word is taken (and which it duplicates, represents, extends, and abstracts).

The bodily-organized word-mind (spoken, sung, written, pictured, and however duplicated, represented, extended, abstracted, and, altogether, concretely rendered) is the source of all art.

All art is the concrete perceptual animation of the responsive word-mind—or the vibratory, sensory, and conceptual event of conditionally arising awareness.

Therefore, percept and concept are the primal substances of all art—and even science is subordinate to every art of means.

The perceptual (or however plastic) aspect of all art is the sensory (and, altogether, vibratory) animation of the intrinsic "self"-apprehension of order.

The perceptual (or however plastic) aspect of all art is the sensory animation of the impulse to either control or escape or transcend evident chaos by means of the exercise of the intrinsically self-evident inner integrity (or root-indivisibility) that is self-apprehended within the human being and in the (thereby apprehended) fundamental order of the humanly observed world.

The conceptual aspect of all art is the mental animation of the intrinsic self-apprehension of order.

The conceptual aspect of all art is the mental animation of the impulse to either control or escape or transcend evident chaos by means of the exercise of the intrinsically self-evident inner integrity (or root-indivisibility) that is self-apprehended within the human being and in the (thereby apprehended) fundamental order of the humanly observed world.

The animation (or the perceptual and conceptual exercise) of the means of art (or, otherwise, of science) is the principal, and profoundly fragile, and (yet) intrinsically indivisible and indestructible response whereby the intrinsic inner integrity (or root-indivisibility) of the human being confronts evident chaos (or internally and externally observed disorder).

Thus and thereby (and thereas), by any effort of perceptual and/or conceptual means, the intrinsic inner integrity (or root-indivisibility) of the human being constantly (but always only temporarily) controls or escapes chaos (through the re-assertion of order), and, ultimately, Perfectly Transcends chaos—by Intrinsically Transcending all perceptual and conceptual means themselves, through the Tacit Self-Recognition of the Intrinsically Self-Evident "Non-chaos" (or the Always Prior Self-Unity, Indivisibility, Indestructibility, and Intrinsic egolessness) of Reality Itself.

III.

Direct Presentation Versus Indirect Representation

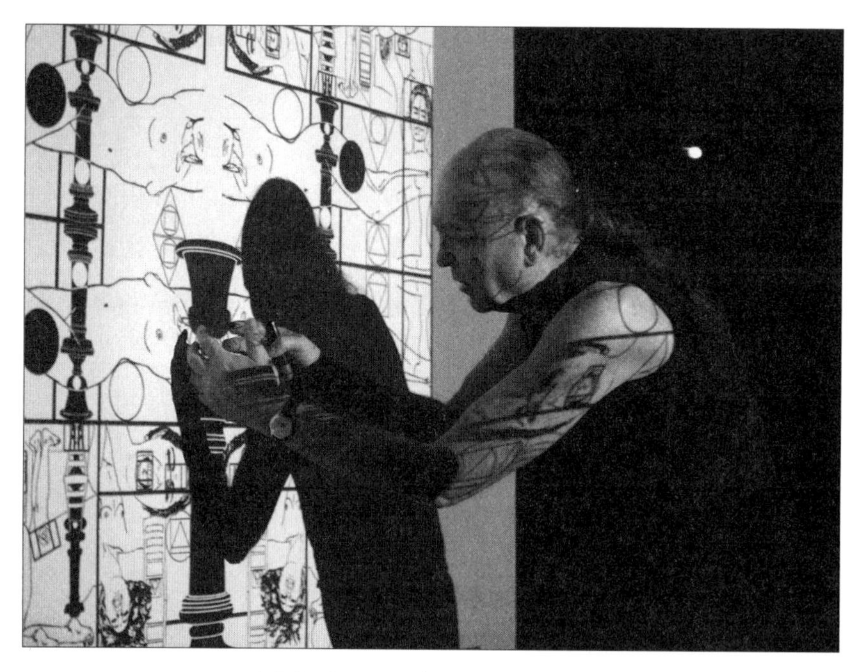

Adi Da Samraj working on *Oculus Two*.

All art is representation—unless the root-cause of representation is (itself) transcended in Reality (Itself).

All art is the reflection of "Narcissus"—unless the psycho-physical illusion of separate (and "self"-reflecting) "self" (or ego-"I") is transcended in the Intrinsic egolessness of Reality (Itself).

The separate "self" (or the ego-"I", or the always "self"-reflecting and intrinsically separate space-time-defined "point of view") and the "objects" (or the mirrored relations) of the separate "self" (or all the "things" and "others" reflected in the mirror of the space-time-defined "point of view") are the only possibilities due to art—unless the separate "self" (or the however represented space-time-defined and all-reflecting "point of view") and the separate "object" (or the reflectively "objectified" relation, or relations) of the separate "self" are (both at once) transcended.

The reflections of "point of view" (or of the total psycho-physical design of the space-time-defined ego-"I") are always representations—or modes of space-time-defined "object", wherein and whereby the otherwise Direct and Intrinsically egoless Self-Presentation of the Intrinsically Indivisible and all-and-All-Transcending Self-Condition of Reality Itself is reduced to the mere ideas and perceptual seemings of apparent space-time-"located" separateness.

The traditional "subject" of artistic representation is either the egoic "self" (which is the "self"-exercise of the "self"-mirroring, all-mirroring, space-time-defined, and, altogether, separate "point of view") or its thereby reflected and (thus) separately defined (or reflectively "objectified") "object"—and, characteristically, even both at once.

The "subject" of even would-be-"non-representational" art is, inevitably and necessarily (by virtue of the mirror's own default), the separate "self" (or the ego-"I", or the "point-of-view-subject") itself.

Therefore, the artistic inevitability of "representation" must be admitted—as long as the intrinsically mirroring (or reflectively "self"-and-"not-self"-"objectifying") nature of intrinsically separate "point of view" is operative in the artistic process of doing (and, otherwise, viewing) works of art.

However, if "point of view" (or the ego-"I", which is the root-cause of all representation) is Really and Priorly transcended, the ritual "objectification" of separate "self" and separate "not-self" (or the "self"-reflected relations of the reflectively "self"-presumed separate "self") is (thus and thereby) transcended.

If space-time-defined (and inherently separate) "point of view" is Really and Priorly transcended, a new artistic possibility emerges—which is the possibility of Direct Self-Presentation (rather than indirect, or merely egoically reflective, ego-reflexive, and even Reality-oblivious representation) of Reality Itself, both Priorly (or As "It" Is) and as "It" appears in and as the intrinsically egoless form and context of any and all modes of conditionally arising happenings.

My image-art (and, also, the literary art I make and do—even, sometimes, within the picture-plane of image-art) is Transcendental Realism, or the Direct (and Intrinsically egoless) artistic Self-Presentation of Reality Itself.

My literary art (or word-art) is the Direct (and Intrinsically egoless) artistic Self-Presentation of Reality Itself via (or in and as) the medium of conceptual meaning.

My image-art is the Direct (and Intrinsically egoless) artistic Self-Presentation of Reality Itself via (or in and as) the medium of perceptual meaning.

Therefore, the artistic (image-art and word-art) work I do is not an exercise (or an artistic transmission) of mere ideas—or, that is to say, of mere mind-reflected (or, altogether, "point-of-view"-made, or ego-made) representations.

If ego-"I" (or "point of view") is Really and Priorly transcended, all representation (or "point-of-view"-mirroring "objectification") is intrinsically transcended—and all apparent experience (or perceptual and conceptual process), and, thus, all doing (and all participatory viewing) of art, is the Direct and Intrinsically egoless Self-Presentation of the Intrinsically Indivisible Self-Condition of Reality Itself.

My art of Transcendental Realism is the Intrinsically egoless (or "point-of-view"-less) Direct Self-Presentation of Reality Itself—As "It" Is.

Therefore, in the Transcendental Realist art I make and do, even what may, in any instance, appear to be "representations" (or "point-of-view"-reflections) of perceptual and conceptual forms are the Intrinsically egoless (or "point-of-view"-less) Direct Self-Presentation of Reality Itself—As "It" Is.

IV.

My Non-Subjective Art of Image

My most fundamental principle of the art of image is non-"subjectivity"—or prior egolessness, intrinsically transcending "point of view", separateness, relatedness, otherness, and all "difference".

On this basis, neither the "internal subject" nor the "external subject" exists (as an irreducibly separate "entity" or "thing")—but both the apparent "internal subject" and the apparent "external subject" exist only non-separately, as merely apparent modifications of the One, and Only, and Intrinsically egoless, and Intrinsically Indivisible, and Perfectly Non-conditional Conscious Light That Is Reality Itself.

My art of image is, intrinsically, neither "expressive" (of "inner subjectivity") nor "representational" (of "outer likeness")—but, rather, the egoless participatory art of image I engage is always showing the tangible event of Intrinsically egoless and Indivisible Reality Itself in apparent conjunction with the otherwise "internal" and "external" elements of (apparently) conditionally arising experience.

My art of image is not merely non-"objective" but also—and primarily—non-"subjective".

My art of image transcends the characteristic of "objectification" of both the "external subject" and the "internal subject".

The image is always realized in participatory response to a "subject" (or "subject-context"), but the image-process is also always "subjectively" egoless (or always already transcending both "point of view" and all internal and external modes of separateness, or "difference").

The "field" of the image (or the meaning-space of overall dimensions, shape, structure, and color) is always (and always priorly) a unified pattern (or a totality of unity), demonstrated as and by means of a formally unified (or self-integrated) whole.

Until the image is thoroughly realized as a formally unified (or self-integrated) whole, it is not yet satisfactory, right, true, final, and complete.

The realization of the final integrity of the image is not "achieved" (as the goal of a seeking-effort), but it is always priorly determined—by the egoless disposition and the elementary formalities (of form, structure, color, and meaning) inherent to the participatory response that spontaneously generates and constitutes the image.

The integrity of the image is made by measure—at and within the image itself. Thus, the integrity of the image is always established by the intrinsic geometries, and the color-force, and the meaning-references of the formal structure (and the constituent forms and elements) on which the image is based (and of which it is comprised, and as which, and by means of which, it is to be both realized and comprehended). Thus, the image is not merely "subjectively" made (or, otherwise, "objectively" purposed), but the image-context is disciplined within itself by forces of measurement that are prior to all "inner" and "outer" likenesses.

Full right realization of the image is a happening determined by necessities that are inherent in the total context of the apparent "subject" and the both spontaneous and intensively formal process of response to the apparent "subject".

Full right realization of the image is a formal happening within and as the totality of all of the characteristics, elements, and constituents of the image-context.

The final (right, true, and complete) realization of the image requires that every fraction (and the whole) of every element and detail of the image (form, structure, color, and meaning) must be formally intended, established, chosen, and controlled—while yet originating in egoless spontaneous participatory response (both to the apparent "subject" and to the image-context itself). Therefore, necessarily, naturalistic (or otherwise "objective") representation of the apparent "subject" (separately, or in, of, and as itself) is neither the goal nor the possibility nor the final result of the image-process.

The image begins in response to the "subject-context".

The image is finally realized (or made complete) in response to the image-context.

The image-context arises in egoless, participatory, spontaneous, and formal response to the "subject-context".

The final (or finally formally realized) image arises as a happening within the ordeal of egoless, participatory, spontaneous, and formal response to the image-context.

Every image has and requires and determines its own particular integrity of form, structure, color, and meaning.

Every image is a non-separate totality, composed of a unified field of non-separate elements in mutual affect.

The generating of any image is a spontaneous action of necessity, "caused" by apparent association with the image-context—or the apparent conjunction with the root-form, root-structure, root-color, and root-meaning that initiates the process in each image-case.

Root-form is primary geometry—square, circle, triangle.

Root-structure is primary geometric integrity—linearity, circularity, angularity.

Root-color is white, black, or any primary color, the inversions of white, black, or any primary color, or the interactions of white, and black, and primary colors, and the inversions of these.

Root-meaning is egoless participation-response.

The generating of any image is a process in egoless participatory response to some apparent "subject" or "subject-context".

The image is not to replicate or "objectify" the apparent "subject" by means of the response.

The image <u>is</u> the response itself—ecstatic, beyond and prior to "point of view", "object", separateness, duality, reflection, and likeness.

In and as the form of the image, the apparent "subject" and the Indivisible Conscious Light That Mirrors the "subject" are non-separately and indivisibly one.

The image is an apparent Self-Modification of the Mirror Itself.

The image is an indivisible and egoless whole—a Self-Portrait of Reality Itself.

V.

Geome and Linead: My Working-Principles of Image-Art

Adi Da Samraj examining a group of Lineads and line drawings while working on *Linead One*.

1. Always Abstraction: Always indicate and respond to the "subject" (or "subject-context") as and via the inherently non-representational and intrinsically self-economized (or always self-simplifying and self-minimalizing) primary geometries ("outer", or gross = square, or linear; "inner", or subtle = circle, or curved; "root", or causal = triangle, or angular, or angled to the image-plane) and/or (possibly) elements made of photographic images (whether whole or fractioned), or of paintings, or of drawings, or of calligraphic script—but, altogether, the image-totality is always to be an abstracted (or visually reduced and simplified, or "essentialized", and self-integrated, or autonomous) form (or image-integrity).

2. Abstract elements are (by means of response to a "subject", or "subject-context") to be assembled into structures of meaning—always in the context of the total surface (or image-whole).

3. The image-form is the single and indivisible image-whole (or totality).

4. The structures within the image-whole are the "cells" of abstract elements that (in modes of shape and color) are the essential energy of meaning-response (or of response to the "subject-context") by which (and as which) the image is to be composed.

5. The image-whole is meaningful form.

6. Meaningful form is always a play upon the intrinsic aesthetic laws of pattern that are inherent to the human brain and nervous system, and that underlie all aspects of human perception, cognition, and action.

7. Meaningful form is a play of pattern-motions—or of relationships between all the elements that are internal to the image-plane and the image-whole.

EDITORS' NOTE: This essay was written by Adi Da Samraj in September 2007, shortly after he completed *Orpheus One* and during the time he was working on *Linead One*. His description of "Geome" and "Linead" as the working-principles of his image-art applies most directly to his work from that time onward—including *Orpheus One*, *Linead One*, *The Goddess of New York*, *The Orphic Font*, and *The Struwwelpeter Suite*. For Adi Da's final summary account of his working-principles, see "The Final Resolution of Geome, Linead, and Orphic Font", pp. 49–66.

8. The formal characteristics of the image-totality are a play between two modes of motion (or of patterning tendency)—the motions that are tending toward symmetry and the motions that are tending toward asymmetry.

9. The finally realized image-whole is a balanced resolution of the inherent conflict between symmetry and asymmetry—but the balance may, itself, be a form that is either dominantly symmetrical or dominantly asymmetrical, depending, in either case, upon the characteristics of the "subject-context" of original meaning that must always govern the motions of the responsively-generated image-totality.

10. Within the formal (or meaningfully formalizing) elements of the image-play are characteristics of polar opposition in mutual dynamic association—the characteristic of strong intensification versus the characteristic of muting (or subduing) of intensity, the characteristic of revealing versus the characteristic of veiling (or covering, or not revealing), the characteristic of perceptually-indicated happenchance (or of arbitrariness and ambiguity) versus the characteristic of perceptually-indicated root-integrity (or of aesthetic and formal, or otherwise meaningful, order), the characteristic of complexity versus the characteristic of simplicity, the characteristic of multiplicity versus the characteristic of singleness, and so on.

11. The finally realized image-whole is, necessarily, a unified whole, a perceptual order that is characterized by an equanimity that demonstrates a realized balance of and between (or in the context of) all the opposites within the meaning-field and the image-plane.

12. The finally realized image-whole is, necessarily, a perceptual demonstration of (both) the root-principle of the prior unity of all conditionality and the Transcendental Principle of the Primal Equanimity of Reality Itself—rather than a mere conventional-reality representation of a yet unresolved experience of ordinarily apparent

disunity, egoic separateness, disturbance, dilemma, struggle, suffering, mortality, and (altogether) the absence of Transcendental Self-Illumination (or of the Intrinsic Self-Realization of the egoless and Indivisible Conscious Light of Reality Itself).

13. The image must not be reduced to mere abstraction—or pattern only.

14. The image must not be reduced to mere representation—or replication of the conventionally "real" (or merely familiar).

15. The image must exist within the plane of meaning—between and beyond both representation and abstraction.

16. The meaning of the image is not its degree of reproduction (or representation, or reflection) of the "objective subject" (or the apparently "objective" context that is the would-be "subject" of the image-making and image-doing response).

17. The meaning of the image is not the reproduction (or representation, or reflection, or even the expression) of the "self-subject" (or the artistic maker and doer) of the image.

18. The meaning of the image is the experiential evidence of the degree of coincidence (or mutual participation) of the "objective subject" and the "self-subject" in the same space—such that both the "objective subject" and the "self-subject" are transcended in and by Means of the Indivisible Singularity of the Perfectly Subjective Space That Is Reality Itself.

19. The image must exist in the Real Transcendental Space That Is always already Perfectly Prior to "point of view".

20. The image must be intrinsically meaningful—but not recognizable (or identifiable merely by reference to a "subject", or "subject-context", outside itself).

21. The image must be utterly free in and as itself—independent of memory and the conventions of ordinary perception.

22. The image must be made and done in response to a perceived or otherwise apprehended "subject" or "subject-context".

23. The making and doing of the image must persist, until the aesthetic ecstasy that demonstrates and proves the finality and wholeness of the image is fully and unambiguously evident.

24. The "Geome" and the "Linead" are to be the principal visual elements in the image-art I now, and hereafter, make and do.

25. The "Geome" is the formal geometric abstract—essentially rectilinear, triangular, and circular—or the forms and structures made of geometric primaries, indicated by line and/or color.

26. The "Linead" is the free-line abstract, that I draw by hand and progressively compose within the specific image-context.

27. The Geome and the Linead are to be freely combined and mutually composed, in intrinsically (or both aesthetically-based and feeling-intuitively-based) meaningful modes of color, form, and structure.

28. The Geome and the Linead are the primary polar opposites of visual energy that I will allow to "play" the images I responsively and spontaneously make and do in egoless space and time.

29. The every image I thus make and do is to be allowed to grow (or to freely develop) in time and space—like a tree within a living forest.

30. The every image is, thus, to be allowed to grow (or to freely develop) until it achieves wholeness and meaningful integrity—or the Perfect Moment of True Form.

VI.

The Root-Subject and The Root-Language of My Image-Art

The fundamental impulse that moves the process whereby I make and do image-art is purposed to render the simplest abstract understanding of perceptually indicated experience—and, in that process, to tangibly manifest that rendering in the intrinsically egoless (and, thus, not "point-of-view"-bound) context of Reality Itself.

Therefore, the fundamental "subject" of every work of image-art I would (thus) make and do is itself always already a simplest abstraction of all possible perceptually indicated experience.

The fundamental "subject" is not any particular phenomenal and "objective" event or other or experiential circumstance.

The fundamental "subject" is the primary simplest form of all possible perceptually indicated experience.

The fundamental "subject" is not mere pattern—but it is mere and primary form.

The fundamental "subject" is the primary complex Geome—the essential linear, curvilinear, and angular shape—formed in any mode of its possibility, and combined with any characteristics of possible perceptual noticing.

The fundamental "subject" is the simple (or, otherwise, combinatory) square and/or circle and/or triangle—responsively extended into a singular and indivisible shape and texturing by means of the energy of the Linead (in any of its possible renderings) and the textures of immediate perception (in any of its possibilities of direct experience).

Therefore, it is not necessary (even though it may also, sometimes, occur) to first render an "objective" root-image (based on meaningful perceptually indicated experience) before the image-work of Geome and Linead can begin to generate the ultimate abstract forms of responsive image-art.

It is only necessary to directly respond to any immediate "subject-context" of perceptually indicated experience, and, on that basis, to immediately move to render an image that is made and done in and as the any responsive mode of Geome and Linead (and any other visual element) that occurs in the moment.

Such is the process now of all the image-art I make and do—and no image thus made and done requires any further explanation, or any other means intended to conform (or otherwise explain) the image in terms of the conventions and the conventional recognizability of "point-of-view"-based and otherwise "ordinary" experience.

Abstraction is, itself, the root-context and the root-language of all perceptually indicated experience—and, therefore, the play of Geome and Linead is the abstract root-context and the root-language of the image-art I am moved and purposed to make and do.

Accordingly, in the process of generating the image-art I make and do, I do not always or necessarily make "naturally" (or otherwise conventionally) recognizable root-images as a preliminary to later (or subsequent) abstract (Geome, Linead, and otherwise rendered) image-forms—but, rather (as a general rule), I make and do image-art always directly and immediately (and always responsively) in the abstract mode itself—and even primarily in the root-language of Geome, Linead, and other associated modes of free-imagery (either with or without direct references to otherwise presumed "objective" visual experience).

Thus, the image-art I make and do is, characteristically, in the mode of responsive abstraction—primarily in the essential root-language of Geome and Linead, and, otherwise and additionally, in other free-image modes, and all of this either in and of itself, as inherent primary "subject", or "subject-context", or else in immediate response to any other perceptually (or otherwise) apprehended "subject", or "subject-context", that I may or may not indicate or describe by title or form.

VII.

The Final Resolution of Geome, Linead, and Orphic Font

Adi Da Samraj creating brush-drawn Lineads
for use as part of the Orphic Font "alphabet"
in *The Struwwelpeter Suite, Part Seven.*

1.

The twentieth-century avant-garde was, as a general principle, working to go beyond the tradition of perspectival and explicitly representational imagery, which has been the Western ideal for the last five hundred years and more. The twentieth-century avant-garde produced many new modes and kinds of image-process relative to the perspectival characteristics of the image itself—but, nevertheless, "point of view" (or the bodily perceiving and spatially-defined ego-"I") itself yet remained as the fundamental basis for both the making and the viewing of images. I am working, in a unique and distinctive fashion, on the fundamental root-issue of going beyond the spatial and bodily "point of view" (and ego-"I") basis of conventional image-making.

The image-art I make and do is, necessarily, abstract in its form—as was generally the case with twentieth-century avant-garde art, and as was finally epitomized by the so-called "abstract expressionist" school (the last of the truly avant-garde visual-art movements of the twentieth century). However, whereas the "abstract expressionist" movement was, like the "impressionist" movement of the nineteenth century, essentially a "painterly" school of image-making, I am moved to an essentially non-"painterly" and technically precise "state of the art" aesthetic.

The image-art (both flat-form and sculptural) that I now (and would in the future) make and do includes fine-drawn and brush-drawn lines and forms and structures that I render by hand and that are, subsequently, electronically (or digitally) re-rendered in large scale, and I combine these with other likewise clear and precise but entirely electronically (or digitally) rendered forms of line and structure and color form that I generate in studio, and I compose all of this as a single whole by intensively making and doing an overall and indivisible surface-structure that is clear and precise in every detail and that is, nevertheless, perfectly free as a whole and in every part. Therefore, in order to accomplish the unique requirements of this mode of non-"painterly" and both technically precise and free aesthetic, I use (and must, necessarily, use) new (twenty-first-century) "state of the art" technical compositional and material-fabrication methods, rather than the traditional "state of the art" conventions and technical means of the past.

When I was concentrating in photographic work, I established an approach to image-making which transcended the inherent limitations (or fixed characteristics) of the camera as a "point-of-view"-machine. The camera literally makes images from a spatially-defined "point" of "view". In that respect, the camera very much epitomizes the Western tradition that has persisted since the Renaissance, wherein there was a transition from a culture oriented toward the Divine (or the Reality beyond "self") to a culture oriented toward the "self"-position of the human being. When the relatively non-ecstatic (or even anti-ecstatic, or "self"-directed and ego-bound, rather than "self"-transcending and, altogether, ecstasy-oriented) culture of humanism (and, eventually, scientific materialism) appeared, the method of perspective came along with it—in which "point of view", or ego-"I", became the basis for structuring images.

I may yet (sometimes) continue to make photographs (mostly as a kind of preparatory sketchbook), and to respond to them (or otherwise use them) in the process of making and doing image-art—but, as a general rule, I am now involved in a thoroughly non-photographic kind of image-process, a process of making images in direct and intrinsically non-perspectival response to the "subject". Therefore, the "point-of-view"-machine I am dealing with now is not the camera but the human body. As the technical basis for constructing images, I am now directly and intensively dealing with the conventions and limiting tendencies of human bodily perception itself. Thus, I am now working on finally resolving all issues relative to the image-making process which have to do with transcending the structuring-force of the conventional and ego-based uses of the body as a perceptual mechanism.

Conventional visual art—and even all of twentieth-century (and, now, twenty-first-century) avant-garde art—uses the "point-of-view"-machine of the human body as the basis for image-making. A fundamental aspect of what I am doing technically is dealing with how the perceiving-body (or ego-driven body-mind-complex) structures perception—and, therefore, how the perceiving-body (or ego-driven body-mind-complex) structures the image-making process. It is in this sense that the image-art I make and do is the new avant-garde.

Beginning especially with the *Spectra* suites, I have been progressively developing an entirely new form of technical approach to image-making. In each succeeding suite, there has been a further advance in the development of an image-making process that intrinsically transcends the human body as a "point-of-view"-based perceptual mechanism, and (thus and thereby) liberates the image-process into the free-domain of egoless coincidence with Reality Itself.

When an image is made from the "point of view" of the body (or of the bodily perceiver), everything is constructed perspectively—or with specific reference to that "point of view", or that viewer. Not only perspectivally-constructed imagery but also representational imagery of all kinds is a result of the conventional use of the body as a "point-of-view"-machine. Thus, every humanly (and, thus, bodily) constructed image tends to contain and encode visual "pointers" that indicate the bodily position and the body-based (and mind-based) "self"-idea (or egoic "self"-identity) of the presumed perceiver (either as artist or as viewer).

I have been working, image by image, on how to use the natural human mechanism of the bodily-perceiving process in a new (and intrinsically egoless) manner, such that the perceptual mechanism no longer enforces a conventional, or perspectival, or "point-of-view"-referring, or representational, or otherwise egoic mode of image.

Thus, I am working on a mode of image-making that is becoming more and more profoundly abstract, in the sense of transcending the "point-of-view"-based use of perception—such that the images I make and do are Transcendental Realism in the fullest sense.

At an advanced stage in this developmental process (of transcending the bodily "point-of-view"-machine), I fully established Geome and Linead as the fundamental visual content of the images I make and do—but a resolution was yet necessary relative to the structural basis (or construction-method) of the images. It was necessary to develop an aperspectival method for constructing images—otherwise, the images would inevitably, in some manner or other, make directly recognizable (or imitative, or iconic) references to a bodily (and, also, mentally) visualized "subject" (and, thus, to a "point-of-view"-based method of image-making).

I am constantly working to make images that are neither generated from a "point of view" (or bodily and spatial "location") nor representing a "subject" as seen from a "point of view". The reason for this intention is in Reality Itself—even in the context of bodily perception. That is to say, for example, to stand in a bodily position (or spatial "location") in a room, and to view the room thus and thereby, is *not* to see the room as a totality (or as it *is*). To see the room as it *is* would require the ability to *simultaneously* view the room from every possible "location" in space and time. The room—as it *is*—*cannot* be seen from a "point of view". Nevertheless, the room itself—as it *is* (or in and *As* Reality Itself)—exists. Therefore, the image-art I am always working to make and do would reveal—in the artistic perceptual language of vision—the "room itself" (or Intrinsically egoless Reality Itself), even in the mode and case of any and every particular "subject".

In order for the Geome and Linead forms to truly transcend the "point-of-view"-machine enforcement that the body makes, there must be a systematic aperspectival approach to how the Geome and Linead forms are structured within the any image. The development of this systematic method of aperspectival structural approach is the final issue relative to the image-making process in which I am involved.

The development of a systematic (and, yet, artistically flexible and free, and not merely mechanical) aperspectival structural approach in the visual arts is, in some respects, analogous to the development of atonality pioneered by Schoenberg and others, in the musical avant-garde of the twentieth century. Schoenberg, in particular, developed a systematic method of using the twelve tones of the chromatic scale, in a manner that could replace (or at least stand along with) the traditional harmonic basis for music-making.

In image-making, there is a tendency of perception to see everything as what could be called an "iconic representation". Indeed, "point of view" *makes* (or originates and enforces) representation—

and "point of view" is (therefore) intrinsically iconic. Thus, bodily perception characteristically makes the "subject" an icon—a representational form seen from a "point of view". I am working to transcend the characteristics of perspectival art (or "point-of-view"-art, or ego-art)—by transcending representational form, or iconic form, and by transcending the bodily enforcer (or "point-of-view"-machine) that would otherwise originate and enforce representational, or iconic, form. Therefore, I am working on an aperspectival—or aniconic—method for making images.

As the basis for the suite entitled *The Orphic Font*, I made a "substitute alphabet", by drawing Linead forms in 26 character-groups, corresponding to the letters of the Latin alphabet. Here and there, the shapes of the Orphic Font characters are, to some degree, suggestive of the traditional letters of the Latin alphabet. However, fundamentally (and, otherwise, in the process wherein I use the Orphic Font as a means to construct images), the Orphic Font characters do not, as a general rule, directly (or, in most cases, even at all) resemble the traditional letters of the Latin alphabet. Indeed, potentially, the Orphic Font characters could be of virtually any kind or shape—and it is, therefore, only necessary that some kind of form or shape be placed in each of the 26 positions that correspond to the letters of the Latin alphabet (and, potentially, even other symbols, such as numbers, punctuation marks, and so forth).

Beginning with the suite entitled *The Orphic Font* (and, most intensively and completely, with *The Struwwelpeter Suite*, the suite that immediately followed it), I have been employing the Orphic Font (which I constantly make anew) as a technical device for image-making, by allowing the words of the image-title to be the visual basis for making the image-structure itself. Instead of writing the words of the suite title in the Latin alphabet, I "spell" the title in the Orphic Font (or "substitute alphabet")—thereby generating the visual structure of the any image, by means of what could be called a "collage of pictographs". Thus, this image-making process is one of choosing a "subject", giving the "subject" a verbal reference, and (then) letting the words of that verbal reference select (from an Orphic Font I make in advance) the image-sources I will freely combine to construct the image (in response to the "subject"). In other words, I am formally limiting the visual form to what the chosen words referring to the "subject" determine (via their transformation into the figures of the Orphic Font). For example, if the "subject" were a boat, I would only use (or spontaneously combine and configure) the "pictographs" for "b", "o", "a", and "t" from the Orphic Font.

Some images I make by this method may include (or, at least, seem to include) recognizability-references, whereas others may seem to be totally non-familiar (or without recognizability-references). In any case, I am making "word-pictures"—or images based on word-"pictographs", rather than on bodily "point-of-view"-perceptions—and the word-"pictographs" do not, as a general rule, directly represent (or directly imitate) the "subject" itself. Thus, I use words (whether of the title or of some other verbal reference I choose) as the means of selecting (from the Orphic Font) the group of intrinsically non-representational Linead forms that I will use (along with various Geome elements) as the essential visual discipline in making that particular image.

The Geome forms that I place into any such image include the outer shape of the field. As a principal image-characteristic, I also often introduce Geome forms (as primary meaning-shapes) into the field of the image. Apart from that, the Linead lines and forms taken from the Orphic Font are, as a general rule, the entire visible basis for constructing the image. When I place these various Font-forms in coincidence with one another, I spontaneously—in response to the original "subject", and (otherwise) in response to the structure itself as "subject"—combine them in various ways, to abstract them further in their coincidence with one another. Also, I sometimes use the particular number of words or letters in the title (or else a number related to some other descriptive verbal or, otherwise, numerical reference to the "subject") as a method of structural measurement (or structural divisioning) within the image-form. In this manner, I thoroughly develop all of the formal elements of the image-structure.

When I have finally established the structure of an image, then, within the structure defined by the however combined Linead (or

Orphic Font) forms and Geome forms, I also (sometimes) introduce other Geome patterns—grids of various kinds, including rectilinear grids of vertical and horizontal lines, curvilinear grids of dots and circles, angular grids of diagonal lines, and so forth. Also, sometimes (even simultaneous with the foundation-process of establishing and combining the Linead, or Orphic Font, lines and forms with the Geome forms) I introduce (and often modify) letters of the alphabet, and various numerical or mathematical signs, and grammatical signs, taken from conventional graphic fonts (such as the ubiquitous Helvetica). Thus, within the image-areas defined by the Linead and Geome structures (made on the basis I have described), there are (frequently) also rectilinear, curvilinear, and angular (or diagonal) Geome elements, as well as other signs. The most fundamental purpose of these grid-elements and sign-elements is (along with all the other image-elements) to serve the purpose of unifying the total field of the image, such that the image-totality—and not any separate element within the image-field—is the one and indivisible and necessary context of viewer-participation in the any such image I make and do.

Characteristically, I use monumental (or larger-than-human-body, and as-big-as-the-viewing-space-will-allow) scale in the material fabricating of virtually all the image-art I make and do—and this as a means of counteracting the viewer's tendency to enclose and "objectify" and control the image, by reducing the image to the bodily (or altogether psycho-physical) and egoic scale of the viewer's "point of view". Nevertheless, when an image is structured using the method of "pictographic word-collage", and (thus) entirely on the basis of Geome forms and Linead forms—characteristically, without any recognizable representational forms—then the image is intrinsically abstracted beyond the ability of the viewer to control it on sight. That is to say, "point of view" is <u>intrinsically</u> transcended in the original structuring of (especially) the finally resolved image-art I make and do, such that the any image cannot, by any means, be contained, avoided, reduced, or limited by the viewer's "point of view". Thus, the monumentality of scale I maintain is an extension of the intrinsically non-containable characteristic of the image itself—rather than a means for achieving that status for the otherwise containable image.

The principles, in summary, are these:

1. The Orphic Font provides the root-system of image-construction.

2. Geome and Linead provide the root-characteristics of visual content.

3. All of the image-elements—including line, shape, and color—are rendered in such a manner that they each have equal force in relation to each and all of the other image-elements.

4. Principal means for equalizing all the elements internal to the image include monochrome (or otherwise color-limited) fields, a limited color-palette (generally, black, white, and either the three primary colors or the seven-color spectrum, either as a whole or in part, with cyan often replacing green), the limiting of colors (other than the monochrome, or otherwise color-limited, field or fields) to the internal lines (or, sometimes, the internal forms or shapes), and the in-filling of all (or most) areas of form or shape with geometric grids (and other signs).

5. The meaning-force of the image is in its indivisible structural totality, rather than in any particular or apparently separate image-element or group of image-elements within the image.

6. There need not be any recognizability-references whatsoever—although many kinds of signs and ciphers and conundrums may be used to serve the meaning-force of the indivisible image-totality and its characteristic of egoless coincidence with Reality Itself.

7. The image is intrinsically anegoic—or not ego-based, or ego-useful.

8. The image is intrinsically non-representational, aniconic, aperspectival, and not limited by bodily or spatial "point of view".

9. The image-art I make and do in accordance with the Orphic Font method is not about either "subjective" or "objective" representation (or "point-of-view"-based illusionism)—but it is about the aesthetic interrelationships between the formal elements themselves, and the ability of that complex and indivisible totality of interrelationships to encode and transmit the tacit force and

characteristic of meaning (or the meaning-response to the particular "subject", apprehended in the context of egoless participatory coincidence with Reality Itself).

10. The image, thus made and done, is, in itself, a unique and indivisible envisionment (or primary, non-dependent, and non-referential vision-state)—rather than a representation of something visible outside itself—and, yet, the meaning-characteristic tangibly encodes the "subject" and transmits its tacit (and profoundly feeling-enabled) meaning-force abstractly (especially via line, shape, and color, rather than via explicit symbol or sign).

11. Because of the technical nature of its form and construction-process, no image made and done in this manner can be pre-imagined—and no such image can (in its totality and in its total particularity of details) be encompassed and contained by memory, or by imaginative reverie, or by conceptual thought.

12. Because of the technical nature of its form and construction-process, every image made and done in this manner can only be spontaneously, immediately, and responsively composed and actualized (and only in the instant of its actual generation, rather than by pre-imagining)—and, thus, only in the image-generating instant of direct response to the "subject" and to the spontaneously evolving and developing context of the internal conjunctions and relationships between the image-elements themselves.

The image-art I make and do in this manner represents the fulfillment, in fullest technical terms, of what I have always intended to accomplish by means of image-art—to create Self-Portraits of Reality Itself, which is to create the art of Transcendental Realism in the purest sense.

Beginning with *Geome One*, all suites include images made (in some cases, even exclusively) of Geome forms. The suites *Orpheus One*, *Linead One*, and *The Goddess of New York* all include images made (in some cases, even exclusively) in the mode of both Geome and Linead. What is added in and after the suite entitled *The Orphic Font* is the systematic application of the Orphic-Font-based aperspectival, or aniconic, construction-method—which systematically (and, thus, by means of a unique abstraction-method) intrinsically transcends the "point-of-view"-orientation of the perceiving body.

The images made in accordance with these principles—of Geome, Linead, and Orphic Font—are, in some sense, a combination of word and image. However, it is not a matter of "word" in the sense of the verbal mind—because I have replaced the speech-based alphabet with abstract visuals that, as a general rule, do not themselves verbally spell out (or otherwise directly "picture") speakable or readable words. The Orphic Font forms are not visual equivalents for speech-based language—and, neither are they explicitly representational visuals. The Orphic Font forms are intrinsically pure abstractions. Thus, the words that I would use to describe the "subject" to which I am responding are simply the formal basis for selecting abstract visuals that have no direct reference to verbal-mind thinking or otherwise representational meaning.

There are, as a general rule, no actual words, as such, in the images (although, for various reasons of meaning, I sometimes include an "I"-indicator, or even some other abstractions made from alphabetical shapes). The Orphic Font forms are visuals that are intrinsically non-representational and aniconic. Therefore, the any image that is made in this manner is necessarily aperspectival and anegoic (or non-egoic), because the perceiving-body, or spatial "point of view", is not the basis for generating the image through a representational connection to a "subject".

The image-making process I have developed is a means of going beyond the ego-based limitations of conventional verbal language, and (also) the ego-based limitations of conventional visual language—and, altogether, the limitations of the ego-based "language" of the perceiving body itself.

Perspectival perception enforces egoity—and vice versa: Egoity enforces perspectival perception, or "point-of-view"-awareness.

The transcending of "point-of-view"-awareness is Transcendental Realism—which is the process associated with intrinsically egoless coincidence with Reality Itself (or the direct apprehension, or apperception, of the Intrinsically egoless Self-Condition of Reality Itself).

Reality Itself is intrinsically aperspectival, anegoic (or non-egoic), aniconic, and non-representational.

Representation (and all recognition of the familiar) occurs from "point of view" only.

Apart from "point of view", there is no bodily-based or spatially-based recognizability, or familiarity, or memory-bondage.

Apart from "point of view", There Is Only Reality Itself.

Thus, the image-method I have been developing—and have now, in every fundamental sense, resolved—is about entirely transcending the ego-based perception that is the conventional basis of image-art. The images I make and do on the basis I have herein described are, in the fullest sense, modes (and perceptually suggestive means) of direct apprehension (or apperception) of the Intrinsically egoless Self-Condition of Reality Itself.

The ability to make image-art that is Transcendentally Real, that is about egoless coincidence with Reality Itself, is what I have been working on for many years. I was doing the same thing in the many thousands of photographic images I have made and done—but I have now gone beyond camera-based imagery, to finally resolve these issues through a systematic approach of establishing a directly responsive and (yet) purely abstract and thoroughly aperspectival (or intrinsically "point-of-view"-transcending) image-process.

The working-method I have developed uses word-symbols that suggestively relate to the verbal (and, thus, conceptual) mind, but the method itself intrinsically transcends the verbal (or conceptual) mind by abstract and entirely "pictographic" means. That same working-method also intrinsically transcends the perceptual mind, by using the Orphic Font "pictographic" method to bypass the otherwise perspective-enforcing, or representation-enforcing, mechanism of body-perception that is actually and in effect a form of ego-enforcement, or ego-visioning.

I have come to the point of resolution of how to do all of this purely abstract image-work systematically, such that there is no reliance on the making of representational forms—whether through outer perception or through inner mental reverie. Thus, not only sense-based representation but also psychological and psychic representation is transcended in this image-making process. Therefore, both conventional realism and conventional surrealism (or egoic "self"-projection) are transcended in this approach. The any image made in this manner is not a picture of what is externally perceived, and it is not a picture of what is internally envisioned or perceived. Instead, the any image made in this manner intrinsically transcends—and, in some cases, for meaning-purposes, purely abstractly uses—all aspects ("outer" and "inner") of the "point-of-view" machine (or tendency) of the body-mind.

The viewer will always tend to exercise a "point of view"—but the viewer of the image-art I make and do will be confounded (and, hopefully, served to the degree of true aesthetic ecstasy) by the "point-of-view"-less characteristic of the image-art. Such is the intention I have in making image-art—to draw the viewer into egoless (or "point-of-view"-less) participation in Reality Itself.

After the completion of *The Goddess of New York*, the outstanding issue was this: how to make images directly, in Geome and Linead forms, without necessarily having to introduce some kind of recognizability (or representational imagery), or (otherwise) without having already (or as a first step) made an image with representational or recognizable forms in it. In other words, the issue was how to make an image in the purely abstract manner, without it being mere pattern—or what I call "wallpaper". That is the issue that I have now resolved, by means of the Orphic Font approach to formal image-construction.

In *The Orphic Font* suite, the diptych entitled "Death Is Light Sans Serif and No 'I'" could be said to be the turning-point image—in which I demonstrate exactly what I have herein described. I have made this diptych with two starkly different images—one with some recognizable elements in it (even though the image is, nevertheless, entirely abstract), and the other with no recognizability-references of any kind. Thus, this diptych shows the transition into the systematic approach of (as a general rule) exclusively using Geome and Linead forms, and dropping the necessity for recognizability, or for any kind of representational forms. The Geome and Linead forms, formally structured by the Orphic Font, are pure abstraction—but they are not mere pattern (or "wallpaper"). This image-art is abstraction that demonstrates and serves (or facilitates) egoless participation in Reality Itself—and, yet, functions within the visually perceptible meaning-field of human awareness.

In any image-art I make and do, there will always be some kind of "subject" to which I am responding—but the image-work will always be a Transcendental Realist response, not a strategically perspectival (or ego-based and merely "nature"-imitating) response. The image-work will, as a general rule, be aperspectival, anegoic, aniconic, and non-representational—and, yet, in the case of every image, there will be a "subject" to which I am responding. Therefore, the any image I thus make and do cannot be mere pattern, or "wallpaper".

The image-art I make and do in this purely abstract form yet has all the characteristics of aesthetic resolution—form, line, structure, color, and so forth—in the context of the meaning-response to a "subject". Thus, the any image I make and do can be enjoyed entirely and simply as the "aesthetic experience" of "significant form" in the mode of pure abstraction—and the viewer is always called and welcomed to enter into the event of the image to even any greater degree of meaning and of ego-transcending (or "point-of-view"-transcending) Reality-Apprehension.

To come to this point of pure (and, yet, tacitly meaningful) abstraction required many years of intensive work on the issues relative to transcending the "point-of-view"-machine of the perceiving-body. That is what I have been working on in the image-making process for decades—and this Geome, Linead, and Orphic Font method is how I am actively resolving it.

2.

Non-recognizability is fundamental to the image-process I have now fully established, beginning (most fully) with *The Struwwelpeter Suite.*

A natural (or representational) view necessarily implies a "point of view". Thus, representational form is, inherently and inevitably, "point-of-view"-imagery. Indeed, representational form <u>enforces</u> a "point-of-view"-mode of image-making—and such a mode of image-making is precisely what I have been working to go beyond. Therefore, in the image-art I am now making and doing, I have completely dropped everything to do with the representational effort.

In the image-art I am now making and doing, whatever is comprehensible only from a "point of view" is entirely absent from the imagery. Thus, in the image-art I am now making and doing, it is not any particular visual element (or elements) in the image, but (rather) the image-totality that is the image. For this to be the case, there must be a kind of "equalization" of all of the elements in the image—and such "equalization" requires the absence of any overtly recognizable imagery, because, as soon as there is any overtly recognizable form in an image, that form "stands out" against everything else in the image, and (thereby) enforces "point of view". Therefore, a fundamental and essential characteristic of the images I am now making and doing is that "point of view" has been utterly eliminated as the basis on which the images are established. Thus, every shape or form within the any image must be "equal" to every other shape or form within the image. Everything "equalizes" everything else—and that "equalization" removes all suggestion of "point of view" as the reference for the image.

Therefore, in the any image I am now making and doing, the imagery is inherently non-recognizable—and the image-totality (rather than a collection of separate elements within the image) is the communicated meaning-force.

While the imagery is inherently non-recognizable in any direct and specific sense, it is (of course) the case that any image-shapes (of whatever kind) can be viewed in such a manner as to suggest recognizable forms—just as people may look at the clouds in the sky and see images in them. Indeed, the potential of seeing recognizable forms in what is, intrinsically, non-recognizable imagery is an essential dimension of the meaning-force of the images I make and do. When viewing the images I now make and do, people can always respond to shape, line, and so forth, and feel that something recognizable is being suggested—but, in actuality, there is no recognizable-from-"point-of-view" form in the imagery. Such is the paradoxical nature of the images I now make and do—with the result that, if the viewer truly enters into feeling the image, the depth of conscious awareness is played upon in a mysterious fashion.

Every image I now make and do is a totality—a total surface without separate parts that stand out from the rest of the parts.

Nevertheless, if the viewer looks at all the details of the any image, he or she may responsively feel that certain details "look like" something. On the one hand, such a response is a right aspect of true participation in the image. On the other hand, the sense of recognizability is also immediately confounded. As soon as one feels that something about the any image is recognizable, one is simultaneously aware that it is, in actuality, entirely non-recognizable. Thus, the mind (or feeling-disposition) of "recognizing things" is simultaneously played upon and confounded. That simultaneous suggestiveness-of-recognizability and confounding-of-all-recognizability, in the same instant, is a fundamental aspect of right participation in the image-art I now make and do. That paradox of apparent recognizability versus utter non-recognizability creates the impact of going entirely beyond "point of view" (or egoic existence altogether). Thus, the fundamental meaning-force of the images I now make and do is ego-transcending (or "point-of-view"-less) participation in Reality Itself.

In Reality Itself, there is always already (or Intrinsically) no ego, no "point of view". Therefore, anything that is about "point-of-view"-recognizability in the context of the natural life is intrinsically a fabrication and a limitation—and, ultimately, a source of binding illusion (or "self"-delusion). This understanding of the Intrinsically egoless (and, thus, "point-of-view"-less) State of Reality Itself is the basis upon which I have worked to make and do aperspectival image-art that thoroughly transcends "point of view".

To presume a "point of view" is inherently a form of abstraction, a form of artifice. However, it is, paradoxically, an abstraction in the form of representation.

Reality Itself is Perfect Abstraction, always Prior to the act of abstracting. Reality Itself is always Priorly Abstract—and, therefore, Prior to the action of de-"objectifying", or of reducing and simplifying, or of (otherwise) relinquishing conformity to already apparent "objective" norms and forms and requirements. Therefore, Reality Itself is without any representational characteristic whatsoever. In Reality Itself, there is not anything that is recognizable. In Reality Itself, there is no separate "anything".

Therefore, the images I am now making and doing contain (as a general rule) no separate "anythings", no recognizable "anythings". It is for this reason that I describe these images as "Self-Portraits of Reality Itself"—or direct exemplifications of the Intrinsically egoless Reality-State of everyone and everything.

Therefore, looking at the images I now make and do should have an impact that confounds "point of view" and suggestively moves people in a manner that (at least tacitly) has something to do with entering into the state of egoless participation in Reality Itself.

To enter into the state of egoless participation in Reality Itself is the import of viewing even any and all of the image-art I have made and done—but, now that I have established a fully resolved mode of the image-making process, this fundamental purpose of the image-art I make and do is served with unique particular force by the utter absence of representational recognizability and of spatial "point-of-view"-references. Thus, I work to move the viewer into the field of the image, and (therein) to play upon the viewer's tendency to confine any particular line or shape to a suggestion of recognizability, and (finally) to move the viewer through that sense of suggestiveness into the realization that he or she is not actually recognizing anything—such that, at last, the image-totality is felt and received as an indivisible whole.

Thus, the images I now make and do are not merely "objective" representations of Reality Itself. Rather, the images I now make and do are an "object"-transcending process for the viewer to enter into, and (altogether) a means for the viewer to tacitly (or non-verbally) participate in the Intrinsically egoless State of Reality Itself. When that perceptually articulated participatory process is effectively engaged, the totality and seamlessness and inherent non-recognizability and indivisibility that are the characteristics of the image become extended and transmitted—such that they tacitly become the characteristics of the actual experiential (and intrinsically "point-of-view"-less) state of the viewer.

VIII.

The Perfect Foreground

The artifice of perspectival image-art constructs (or composes and fabricates) a spatial illusion, based on the projecting of a fixed "point of view" into and onto the field of perception. The effect of this act of projection is the constructing of a spatial configuration that conforms the perceptual field to a pattern that extends the "point of view" toward a vanishing-point (or an horizon, or an iconic "subject"), thereby modeling or configuring the spatial content between the "point of view" and the vanishing-point as if it were a plastic domain intrinsically shaped by the fixed "point of view" (or the separate ego-"I") itself.

This perspectival art-practice—which, previous to the revolution of twentieth-century "modernism", had acquired the virtually judicial force of an obligatory convention of perception, understanding, and culture, especially in the domain of Western art since the Renaissance—extends the ordinary "realism" of bodily and egoic perception into the domain of culture, society, and politics in a would-be normative, doctrinal, and dogmatic manner. The cultural, social, and political effect of perspectival art-practice is the idealization of ego (or the illusion and the separative activity of separate "self") and the desecration (or thorough secularization) of Truth and life, or of Reality (Itself, and altogether).

Both life and art engaged on the basis of the Truth (or As-Is-Force) of Reality Itself is intrinsically egoless (or anegoic, or "point-of-view"-less), non-perspectival (or aperspectival), and always rooted-in-depth (or, that is to say, always Priorly Self-Established in the "foreground", rather than projected toward a vanishing-point, or an icon, or a "background", via a spatial pattern modified in conformity to a fixed "point of view", or a psycho-physically and spatially defined ego-"I").

In perspectivally-based image-art (or egoic and iconic image-art), the vanishing-point (or the horizon, or the "background", or the egoically representational icon) is the principal "subject" (or "subject-location").

In aperspectival art (or anegoic and aniconic art), the "foreground" is the principal "subject" (or "subject-location").

That is to say, the "foreground"—always Prior to the spatially-constructing "point of view" (or egoic perspective)—precedes (or is the always Prior basis) for the process of perception in aperspectival art-practice.

The aperspectival "foreground" is the anegoic and aniconic "root" of Reality-perception.

If the aperspectival "foreground" is made the basis for the making and doing of image-art, the spatial field is neither conformed to a fixed "point of view" nor modeled relative to a vanishing-point—and the result is an image that is thoroughly aperspectival, anegoic, and aniconic.

The aperspectival "foreground" is the "Transcendental Location" of Intrinsic egolessness—or of the Native Reality-Consciousness, That merely Witnesses all arising conditions (rather than reacting and re-coiling into the illusions of separate "self" and its "not-self" opponent).

Image-art that is thoroughly aperspectival, anegoic, and aniconic is Transcendental Realism—or the image-art of egoless coincidence with Reality Itself.

The aperspectival, anegoic, and aniconic "foreground" is the pervasive and <u>only</u> "space" of Transcendental Realist image-art.

The aperspectival, anegoic, and aniconic "foreground" is the "space" of egoless perception, wherein forms arise in paradoxes of mere appearance, shift, and change—without any ego-"I" (or fixed "point-of-view"-base) to construct the happening and think the meaning of it.

Transcendental Realist image-art is the image-art of Reality (Itself, and altogether)—and, as such, it is true (and intrinsically non-religious) sacred image-art, or the Reality-based "holy" image-art of Self-Evident (and Always Priorly "Set Apart") Truth and Beauty.

Transcendental Realist image-art is the true image-art of the "Perfect Foreground".

IX.

The Maze of Ecstasy

1.

During the Renaissance, perspective—or the systematic and "scientifically" rule-based representation of physically-perceived, or (otherwise) mentally-conceived, "subjects" as if they are being observed by a spatially and temporally "point-of-view-located" viewer—became the fixed and idealized basis of Western image-art. When an artistic image is created on the basis of the rules (and the ego-affirming idealism) of perspective, everything in the image points (or refers back) to the viewer—or the "point of view" of ego. Thus, beginning with the Renaissance, "point of view" (itself), or ego (itself), became the root-"subject" and fixed ideal of Western image-art and of the totality of Western culture.

It is an irony that the Western Renaissance—or the historical period that saw the formulation of Copernican cosmology, which asserted the centrality of the Sun, rather than of the Earth—is also the historical period of the assertion of the centrality of Man (and of the egoic individual), rather than any presumption of the Divine, as the essential "subject" of human "knowledge", culture, and history. The Western Renaissance was the birth of human ego-culture—and perspectivally-constructed image-art was a fundamental device and sign of that ego-culture and its idealization of the individuality of "point of view".

Perspectival image-art originated with the analysis of how things appear from the "point of view" of an individual human observer. On the basis of that analysis, the artists of the early Renaissance developed a systematic and mathematically precise method of rendering a painted image as it would otherwise be constructed by the eye of the individual observer. However, it is not merely the physical eye that constructs the perspectival view of the world. Most fundamentally, it is "point of view" (itself), or ego (itself), that constructs the perspectival view. Thus, perspectival imagery represents what ego (or "point of view") makes of the world.

In the conventions of perspectival image-art, the physical eye and the ego-"I" are the same.

The intrinsically ego-transcending root-presumption associated with the image-art I make and do is precisely the opposite of the ego-based and ego-idealizing root-presumption associated with perspectival image-art. Perspectival image-art glorifies the ego's construction of the world—as if that ego-constructed world is (itself) Reality Itself—whereas Reality Itself is always Prior to the ego's construction of a world and Prior to any and every "point of view" within the world.

The world that the ego—or any spatial and/or temporal "point of view"—sees is not how Reality Itself Is. My image-art is based on an aesthetic that is rooted in how Reality Itself Is. My image-art always undermines the "position" of the ego, or the will of the ego to feel that it is "located" in a world of its own construction.

Therefore, the image-art I make and do does not point to—or idealize, and depend upon, and assert the position and the separateness of—the viewer. Indeed, the image-art I make and do is intended to directly counter "point of view", or ego. Thus, the image-art I make and do is both aperspectival and anegoic (or non-egoic). The image-art I make and do is specifically intended to counter the ego's expectation of being able to construct a world.

2.

The advent of perspective in the early Renaissance signalled a profound paradigm shift in European civilization—a shift from a culture centered on the "God"-idea to a culture centered on the human individual, or the ego. In the Middle Ages (and earlier, even back into ancient times), the fundamental "subject" of Western art was the "idea of the Divine"—whereas, beginning with the Renaissance, and lasting until the beginning of the "modernist" period, the fundamental "subject" of Western art was the "idea of the human individual", as conveyed (in particular) by the technical device of perspective. Thus, pre-Renaissance culture was, at root, about surrendering the ego to the "God"-idea, while Renaissance culture was, at root, about the idea of magnifying the "knowledge" and the power of the ego, and about controlling and exploiting the world as constructed by the ego.

The various modes of avant-garde image-art in the "modernist" period arose out of—and, to a greater or lesser degree, in reaction to—the Western tradition of perspectival image-art. Arising out of this background, "modernist" avant-garde image-art *played* on the notion of "point-of-view"-perception—investigating various different modes of making image-art in an apparently non-perspectival manner, modes that were intended to (in one or another manner) break free of "point of view", but, nevertheless, always preserving "point of view" itself as the core "subject". The "modernist" project of achieving liberation from "point of view" (and liberation from the perception of the world constructed by "point of view") never came to a full resolution. Certain core issues remained to be dealt with. Those issues had to do, principally, with how to make art that transcends "point of view" *absolutely*—rather than only partially, or only by the effort of irony and seeming.

The image-art I make and do is the intrinsically ego-transcending (and, thus and thereby, perspective-transcending, or intrinsically aperspectival) image-art that participates in (or egolessly coincides with) Reality Itself.

The image-art I make and do—rather than re-asserting myth-based ideas relative to the Divine (as in the case of pre-Renaissance image-art), or indulging in ego-based glorification of the individual "self" (as in the case of Renaissance-based pre-"modernist" image-art), or, otherwise, merely playing upon the failure of perspectivally-based ego-culture (as in the case of both "modernist" and "post-modernist" image-art)—asserts the intrinsic freedom of intrinsically ego-transcending participation in Reality Itself.

The image-art I make and do directly addresses and (thoroughly and, at last, completely) resolves *all* issues inherent in the consideration of *absolutely* transcending "point of view".

The image-art I make and do is not an art (in the pre-Renaissance manner) of picturing a "God"-idea, or of rendering some kind of visual equivalent of conventional religion. The image-art I make and do is not an art (in the Renaissance manner) about the ego-"I", or about the methods whereby the ego-"I" constructs its version of the world. The image-art I make and do is Transcendental Realism—or the image-art of egoless coincidence with Reality Itself.

3.

There is "God-art", there is "ego-art", and there is "Reality-art".

Pre-Renaissance image-art is "God-art"—or image-art made and done relative to Deity, or deities, or gods and goddesses. Thus, pre-Renaissance image-art is about what the space-time-bound ego presumes to exist above and beyond itself. Therefore, the total image-art tradition of the pre-Renaissance West (extending back into ancient pre-Christian times) is "mythology-art"—principally intended to visually portray the mythology of divinity in one mode or another, including (in later centuries) the Christian mode.

Renaissance image-art and post-Renaissance image-art (up to the "modern" period) is "ego-art"—or image-art specifically designed to portray the ego's view (or "point-of-view"-construction) of "reality", by means of the systematic application of the codified laws of perspective. Even the thoroughly secularized avant-garde Western image-art of the "modern" and "post-modern" era is still a play upon (or a failed effort to escape from) the tradition of "ego-art", or "point-of-view"-art.

The image-art I make and do is "Reality-art"—not in the conventional sense of image-art that imitates or merely reproduces ordinary "reality" (which conventional "reality-art" is another form of "ego-art"), but in the sense of image-art that intrinsically ego-lessly coincides with Reality Itself. Thus, the image-art I make and do is not about myth-based views of Reality, nor is the image-art I make and do about the ego that invents myth-based views of Reality. The image-art I make and do is about Reality Itself—beyond myth, and beyond egoity.

The image-art I make and do has required profound philosophical and Spiritual preparation even to be made—decades of intensive consideration regarding fundamental issues of Truth, of Reality Itself, of the means to go through and beyond all traditional and ego-based modes of thinking and understanding, in order to come to the point where I could make and do image-art on an intrinsically and entirely "point-of-view"-less basis.

4.

I remember going to a particular place at Coney Island when I was a boy. There was a maze of multi-colored posts into which one would enter, walk around, and keep walking into dead ends. In this particular case, there were not only dead-end walls as one would walk around inside this cage of mazes, but there were also mirrors reflecting one as one walked into them, or else reflecting something obliquely, so that one lost one's sense of the space. One would constantly slam into oneself, into one's misunderstanding of the space one was in.

The nature of egoic experience is something like that. It is a maze of misunderstanding of the nature of where one is. One is constantly slamming into oneself, because one does not understand the nature of the space (or the "room") itself.

The apparent world and the ego-"I", or (space-time-"located") "point of view" that "knows" the world of views, are mere conventions of human design. The conventionally apparent universe is a "room" without an exit—an unending maze of shapes and signs defined and limited by the any and every "point of view" that perceives "it". Therefore, the "maze" of universe apparent to ego's "I" cannot be escaped.

All seeking is an egoically-driven effort toward the illusion of escape—either by distraction or by purification or by final fulfillment or by flight to absence. The maze of ego-"I" and the universe of endless and futile seeking cannot be escaped by any means—but the ego-"I" itself, and all of its views of universal "room", can be intrinsically (and, thus, Perfectly) transcended.

Not space-time re-"location", but ecstasy—or the intrinsic transcending of "point of view" and <u>all</u> space-time-"locatedness"—is the only true and possible release from the "maze of room" that is all present bondage to thought and perception. Therefore, the image-art I make and do is made and done to serve true ecstasy by aesthetic means—and, thus, by un-confining every viewer from the shape and place of "point of view".

The images of perspectival art are not merely representations of what is in the world. In perspectival image-art, one is constantly slamming into oneself. The perspectival image—and "point-of-view"-based perception itself—is a kind of maze, in which one does not get the direct (and liberating) sighting of the Reality one is actually in. Rather than seeing Reality Itself, one is always seeing the "point-of-view"-based "reality" one has naively constructed. Therefore, one is constantly getting lost and confused. And, always—no matter how many landscapes, portraits, still lifes, or visual narratives one looks at—all perspectivally-constructed images are essentially about oneself (or the "point-of-view"-bound and space-time-bound perceiving and thinking ego-"I").

When one looks at perspectivally-based image-art, one is constantly being reminded of oneself, constantly being re-"located" in one's own position of presumed separateness. One is, in effect, constantly walking into one's own face. Thus, perspectivally-based image-art is inherently Narcissistic art—regardless of its apparent "subject" matter. Perspectivally-based image-art is, fundamentally, about the egoic "self", or separate (space-time-"located") "point of view". Thus, when viewing perspectivally-based image-art, one is constantly getting lost in a maze of mirrors and fractions, in which one cannot "locate" and understand Reality Itself.

In order to intrinsically "locate" and understand Reality Itself, the maze of "point-of-view"-based perspectival experience must be seen as a whole—or from a "position" Prior to the totality—rather than seen from "inside" (or as a partial view, and as a "point-of-view-located" separateness, trapped within the maze itself).

The image-art I make and do is about intrinsically transcending the maze of ego-based experience by standing "outside" the maze (or by standing in the ecstatic "position", Prior to "point of view"). The image-art I make and do is about not only showing Reality As It Is, but about using the device of images to confound the ego's effort to construct the world and to understand the world in its own image. Through that confounding, the image-art I make and do serves the feelingly-participating viewer in an ecstatic and tacit understanding of Reality Itself, through the viewing of image-art that does not point to "point of view".

I have (over many decades) made all kinds of images, and the various kinds of images each have different purposes. Some of the images I have made and done are apparently in the mode, at least to some degree, of a perspectivally-based representational form of imagery. In this essay, I am summarizing the ultimate nature of all the image-art I have made and done—and, especially, the fully and finally resolved image-art to which the entire process has led.

In all the forms of image-art I have made and done, I have been engaged in a process ultimately leading to imagery that is thoroughly aperspectival and anegoic—or "point-of-view"-transcending in the fullest terms.

5.

Art is always coincident with culture, and culture is invariably bound to tradition—to all the limitations and (otherwise) all the virtues of humankind altogether. A global transformation is now required in human culture—after the devastation, or collapse, of ego-civilization in the twentieth century. Something entirely new is required—something comprehensively right.

My entire life has been spent in working to establish the basis for a "radically" new and "radically" comprehensive culture. My image-art is a summation, in artistic terms, of all the work I have done. Similarly, the books I have written are a summation, in literary and philosophical terms, of that same lifetime work. My lifetime of work has always been about the rightening of human existence and the transcending of what is binding human beings and leading them on a destructive course.

Therefore, the images I make and do—like the books I have written—are intended to establish a new paradigm of human civilization. The images I make and do are about an entirely different—and altogether ego-transcending—mode, not only of picture-making, but of living and understanding.

What is now required is an epochal change in the history of human endeavor. Just as the Renaissance represented a profound summation of transformation in human endeavor, so now a new kind of transformation is happening.

The "modernists" were moving toward this transformation, but they were also making images in the midst of the virtual collapse of world-civilization in the twentieth century. Since that collapse, it is no longer possible to return to a tradition that idealizes the human ego. Indeed, what happened in the twentieth century was the definitive failure of Renaissance-originated civilization, which civilization was based on the idealization and glorification of the ego and on the wholesale adoption of the ego's perspectival view of "reality".

The Renaissance was the collapse of the "God"-civilization that preceded it—the civilization based on mythologized presumptions of what is traditionally conceived to be spatially and temporally "behind" and "above" the world. The Renaissance destroyed that earlier form of civilization. With the Renaissance, "God"-myth-based civilization was replaced with human-based civilization, or ego-civilization—or the civilization based on the myth of the human ego-"I". That ego-civilization came to its essential end in the twentieth century.

In this post-ego-civilization era, the only right basis for human existence—now, and into the future—is the establishment of a civilization that is no longer based on idealization of the ego, but also no longer based on "God"-mythologies. True and right life is neither "God"-myth-based nor ego-based. True and right life is intrinsically ego-transcending. True and right life is the life of intrinsically egoless coincidence with Reality Itself. True and right life intrinsically transcends all mythologies—whether of "God" or of "Man".

The old civilization is ego-based and ego-bound. The old civilization idealized the ego, and it ended with a world of egos destroying one another. That course, in fact, is still happening, and must be stopped—but it cannot be stopped merely by force. A transformation of human understanding and of human processes altogether must occur—on every level, including the artistic level.

6.

When I was doing photographically-based image-art, I was dealing with the fundamental limitations in what has been (and still is, in some shadowy form) governing humankind. I did this by working to transcend the inherent limitations in the "point-of-view"-technology that is materialized as the instrument of the camera. The entire Western tradition of perspectival and ego-based image-art is enshrined in the technology of the camera. The camera is the materialization of "point of view". Thus, the camera is a device that summarizes the ego-based (and, thus, space-time-"point-of-view"-based) civilization of the last six hundred years.

I no longer work specifically with the camera, except to use it occasionally as a kind of sketchbook. Having accomplished what I needed to accomplish in camera-based work, I have now developed a mode of image-process that does not require the camera as a principal means of producing images. However, the images that I am making and doing now are aesthetic modes that came about through the ordeal of working with the "ego-technology" of the camera.

If one rightly approaches the image-art I make and do, the "point of view" (and, thus, all of ego-"I") is confounded. The image-art I make and do is not merely about some kind of punishing of the ego, or some kind of arbitrary frustrating of the viewer—as if the mere sensation of frustration were the purpose of the image-art. Rather, the image-art I make and do is purposed to serve the viewer's transcending of space-time-bondage and "point-of-view"-fixedness (and, thus, egoity itself) altogether—such that he or she can directly tacitly (and by means of aesthetic ecstasy) participate in Reality Itself.

I am not looking to represent ego in some form through the image-art I make and do, or to represent a world of a spatial configuration that ego can comprehend and feel comfortable—or even uncomfortable—with. The image-art I make and do is not a construct made by ego for the ego's purposes.

I have written at length about the image-art I make and do—in order to give fundamental guidance relative to rightly participating in the images and rightly understanding what that right participation is about. Otherwise, there will be an inevitable tendency to view the image-art I make and do in accordance with the prevailing conventions of interpreting art in the "post-modern" world—and such interpretations will inevitably tend to be misinterpretations.

The fully resolved image-art I make and do is a means to directly participate in Reality Itself—and not (in Alberti's language) a "window" through which to view the ego's "point-of-view"-based construction of the world of conventional "reality". The fully resolved image-art I make and do is not about looking through something to something else. Likewise, the fully resolved image-art I make and do is not about looking from a "point of view" into a world constructed by "point of view" (or by perspectival and, altogether, space-time-bound perception). The fully resolved image-art I make and do has nothing to do with "point of view". The fully resolved image-art I make and do does not illustrate anything, and it does not merely reflect the natural characteristics of perception.

Altogether, there is a profound—and even absolute—difference between perspectival image-art and the fully resolved image-art I make and do.

7.

The great process of Reality Itself, the great process of human sanity, is an in-depth process. That process takes place in the depth-domain of awareness, not in the superficial domain of outer awareness. Reality Itself is the in-depth domain that intrinsically transcends ego and "point of view".

"Post-modern" civilization is secular, superficial, materialistic, outward-directed, and "object"-oriented. "Post-modern" civilization is founded on a mode of propaganda about the nature of existence that has driven humankind to the point of self-destruction. The propaganda of scientific materialism is based on the mythology of the ego, the mythology of "point of view". The perspectival method in art is an extension of egoity, a manifestation of the notion that Reality is the appearance that the ego constructs—and scientific materialism is an expression of that same presumption.

The only "reality" scientific materialism is looking at is a construct of egoity, or (space-time-"located") "point of view". Scientific materialism is looking at the "room" seen from a "point of view"—not the "room" as it Always Already Is, inclusive of all possible "points of view" and (thereby) transcending "point of view" itself.

The notion that Reality is reducible to what the ego constructs is inherently "self"-deluded and (at least potentially) insane. The image-art I make and do is made and done in order to serve the transcending of that egoically "self"-deluded (or "point-of-view"-insane) notion. Therefore, right participation in the images I make and do is, necessarily, in-depth, and not superficial.

Right participation in the images I make and do requires one to relinquish—or ecstatically feel beyond—"point of view". The images I make and do are for the purpose of serving the ecstatic transcending of "point of view"—or the intrinsic transcending of the ego-"I"-method, which is the activity of perceiving and, in effect, constructing the world from one's own separate (space-time-"located") "point of view". The images I make and do are images of the "room" (or the world, or Reality Itself) As it Is—or As the "room" itself, and not the "room" as it appears to be from any particular position within it.

Reality Itself requires the surrender and the transcending of all limitations, all "points of view"—in every one's case. Reality Itself cannot be controlled by the ego. Thus, image-art that can be controlled, contained, or comprehended from the perspective of ego (or "point of view") is a convention of egoity itself—and such image-art is, inevitably, a superficial "object" of human diversion.

What is profoundly in-depth is intrinsically egoless. What is profoundly in-depth is not what is merely "inward"—or "inside" the ego. What is profoundly in-depth is not wandering among the ego's "objects". Rather, what is profoundly in-depth is at the true root-depth—altogether Prior to ego-"I", space-time-"locatedness", and "point of view".

At the true root-depth, or the always Prior depth, there is always already no ego. That always Prior depth does not merely perceive through the eye. That always Prior depth ecstatically apprehends the Reality-Nature of the "room" itself—or the world, or Reality Itself, As It Really Is.

The intrinsic ecstasy of Prior and Perfect Depth is the root-basis for a new philosophy and a new way of life—the philosophy, the way of life, and, indeed, the necessary new global human civilization of egoless participation in Reality Itself.

X.

Orphic Magic

1.

All human-made art is a play on (or the "work" of participation in) the method of "magic"—which (in the case and event of human-made art) is purposed to "objectify" (and, thus, "capture") the chosen "subject" in a state (or process) of unity with (or in union with, or in re-union with, or in a state of non-"difference" from) the "self" (of the artist and/or the artist's patron, audience, or favored "other").

All human-made art is a "magical" process, engaged between the "self" (whether personal, impersonal, or collective) and the "subject" that is "objectified" (or "differentiated", or defined, or chosen) by the "self".

If the "self" is the ego-"I", the "subject" of the ego-made art is subordinated to the ego-"I" by means of a "magical" activity of "objectification", wherein and whereby the "subject" is (whether positively or negatively) "known" and controlled by the ego-"I".

The "subject" of any particular example of ego-made art is always either "holy", or "sacred", or "secular", or "profane".

That is to say, the "objects" (or "objectified subjects") of ego-made art are either of a "holy" (or profoundly "set apart") kind, or of an otherwise "sacred" (or positively regarded and "protected") kind, or of a "secular" (or non-"holy", and non-"sacred", but, nevertheless, generally positively regarded, and even "protected") kind, or of a "profane" (or non-"holy", non-"sacred", even "lower" than "secular", and, generally, not altogether positively regarded, and even not at all "protected") kind.

Thus, the "magical" activity of "objectifying" (and, thus, "capturing", or subordinating, and "knowing", and controlling) the would-be "subject" of ego-made art, and of, subsequently, seeking (or "magically working" toward) unity (or union, or re-union) with the "objectified subject" (or of "absorbing", or "assimilating", the "objectified subject" into the egoic "self") is an enterprise that is observable as either a "holy" or a "sacred" or a "secular" or a "profane" activity.

In any case (whether "holy", "sacred", "secular", or "profane"), all ego-made art is a "magical" activity—engaged by an egoic "self" relative to an actively "objectified" (or subordinated, "captured", "known", and controlled) "subject".

All ego-made art is, thus, of an intrinsically aggressive nature—although it can (and, historically, generally does) demonstrate itself in otherwise humanly benign modes of artistic artifacts.

2.

Many devices (or "tools") for the making of ego-based art have been devised throughout the history of human endeavor and culture—now, at least in the interpretations of academicians and intellectuals, divided between the presumed-to-be intrinsically "separate" categories of "Eastern" art and "Western" art.

Those devices (or "tools")—and, indeed, all the traditions and conventions that commonly determine what is and what is not "acceptable" as art—are of very significant import (and they should provide the basic "issues" for the academic study of human-made art).

Among the most fundamental and important devices (or "tools", or "issues") relevant to a right understanding of human-made image-art—and of ego-made image-art in particular—are those of icon and of perspective.

The icon is the "objectified subject", artistically represented in its own likeness.

The artistic method of perspective is the application of a technical rule of "point of view" (or of "self-locatedness") relative to the perceived (or however conceived) "objectified subject" (or icon).

Any icon (or "objectified subject") of ego-made image-art may be represented perspectivally (or in accordance with the technical rules associated with the analysis of "point-of-view"-based natural perception)—but any icon of ego-made art (in any mode or medium of human art-making) may also otherwise be represented non-perspectivally (or by perceptual devices that do not apply the technical rules of analytical perspective, but which, nevertheless, represent the icon, or the "objectified subject", with reference to the ego-"I", or egoic perceiver).

The "subject" of ego-made art is always iconic, and (especially in the domain of visual art, or image-art) thoroughly perspectival (or, at least, non-perspectivally referenced to the ego-"I").

3.

The image-art (and the literary art) I make and do is the intrinsically egoless art of Transcendental Realism.

Transcendental Realist art is the art (or "magic") of egoless coincidence with Reality Itself.

Transcendental Realist art is a mode of art that, necessarily, both tacitly and actively renounces the devices (or "tools") of icon and perspective (or, otherwise, of ego-referencing non-perspectival representation) that otherwise characterize ego-made art.

Transcendental Realist art (as is especially evident in its fullest development and most fully elaborated demonstration) does not egoically "objectify" (or aggressively "capture", "know", and control) its "subject"—Which Is Intrinsically egoless Reality Itself (by whatever medium or mode of sign Reality Itself is, thus, artistically rendered).

Transcendental Realist art is intrinsically egolessly established in always Prior unity (or non-"different" coincidence) with its "subject"—and, therefore, the making and doing of Transcendental Realist art does not involve a "magical" effort (or a search) toward unity (or union, or re-union, or the goal of non-"difference", or even the satisfaction of the root human need for transcendence).

Therefore, I describe the image-art (and the literary art) I make and do not only as "Transcendental Realism" but as "Orphic Magic"—or the artistic (or aesthetic) process of egoless (or ecstatic) participation in the human domain of perception (and all of conditionally arising experience), such that the artistically chosen "subject" and the apparent "self" (or, most simply, the body-mind-complex, or the psycho-physical pattern-mechanism) of perception (and of the entirety of conditionally arising experience) are Tacitly, always Priorly, and Perfectly Transcended in egoless coincidence with Reality Itself (Which Is both Truth Itself and The Beautiful Itself).

XI.

The Self-Discipline of Ecstatic Participation In The Image-Art I Make and Do

Adi Da Samraj photographing a bicycle for use in *Linead One*.

1.

I make images by means of a process of abstraction.

That process of abstraction occurs in two stages.

The first stage is a process of abstraction relative to the totality of the "subject".

That first-stage process of abstraction takes place in feeling-response to the "subject" (with all the dimensions of meaning-force that are inherent in the "subject", whatever they may be in any particular case).

The second stage is a process of abstraction relative to the newly-created abstract image itself.

That second-stage process of abstraction takes place in feeling-response to the image (as a purely abstract visual form, within its own domain of visual elements).

First, there is the responsive abstracting of the "subject"—then, there is the responsive abstracting from or within the abstract image-form itself.

2.

On the one hand, the second-stage abstraction always has encoded within it all the responsiveness to the original "subject"—but, on the other hand, that second-stage process, more and more, goes ecstatically beyond any explicit visual references to the original "subject".

Ultimately, the second-stage process of abstraction goes utterly beyond all referentiality.

The image then becomes its own abstract field (or domain), containing no references beyond itself.

The image is then purely itself.

EDITORS' NOTE: This essay was written by Adi Da Samraj in January 2008, during the time he was creating his final work, *The Struwwelpeter Suite* (Parts I–VII). His description of the two-stage process of abstraction applies most directly to his later work—including *Oculus One*, *Oculus Two*, *Orpheus One*, *Linead One*, *The Goddess of New York*, *The Orphic Font*, and *The Struwwelpeter Suite*. For Adi Da's final summary account of his working-principles, see "The Final Resolution of Geome, Linead, and Orphic Font", pp. 49–66.

3.

To rightly view such an image is to participate in the domain of the image itself.

There are all kinds of meanings encoded in any such image—and anyone who seriously gives himself or herself over to feeling-participation in the image can enter into those meaning-dimensions.

Such feeling-participation is a performance-assisted "subjective" process.

Thus, the depth of the process depends on how profoundly the individual viewer enters into it.

4.

To view one of the second-stage abstractions most profoundly is to enter into the Transcendental Realist Field of the Domain of Reality Itself.

Every image I make and do is a means for serving the viewer's ego-transcending participation in Reality Itself.

The means is simply the image itself—not the image as referring to something else.

Ultimately, the "subject" of any image I make and do is Reality Itself.

True participation in Reality Itself is, necessarily, egoless.

Therefore, true participation in Reality Itself must transcend "point of view".

5.

When I achieve the final resolution of an image, taking into account all of its formal elements, then the process of abstraction has achieved a full and complete resolution.

Then the image exists in its free final form.

6.

To examine the any image I make and do with the intention of seeing what can be said in reference to the presumed "subject" of the image is a secondary process.

That process of examination has its own legitimate interest, of course—but that process of examination is not the fundamental process of truly participating in the any image I make and do.

Ultimately, the true force of the any image I make and do is not a matter of its reference to a "subject".

Rather, the any image I make and do is, primarily, a means of participating in Reality Itself.

7.

It does not make any ultimate difference what "subject" I was originally responding to when I created any image.

Fundamentally, the any image I make and do simply exists as itself, in its own domain.

The any image I make and do has nothing directly to do with the "subject" to which I was originally responding.

The any image I make and do is never an "illustration" of the "subject" to which I was originally responding.

8.

In the any image I make and do, there are references to the "subject", and there are meaning-dimensions that relate (directly or indirectly) to the "subject"—and all such references and meanings are part of the associative mind (or psychic field) of anyone who fully participates in the image.

The responses of the viewer's associative mind (or psychic field) can be supplemented by considering (or even studying) the "subject" to which I was originally responding in making any particular image.

My own response to the "subject" is always in evidence in any particular image, and so there is always something that can be examined or said about all of that.

Every image I make and do always has its own particular aesthetic characteristics—based on meaning-response to the "subject", and (otherwise) based on the process of working with the formal elements of line, form, color, shape, and comprehensively indivisible structure.

However, true participation in the image is, fundamentally, a process of aesthetic ecstasy, a process of transcending egoity.

9.

The process of truly participating in the any image I make and do is without reference to a "subject" perceived from "point of view".

Thus, the process of truly participating in the any image I make and do is, most fundamentally, with reference to Reality Itself—Which Intrinsically Transcends "point of view".

Ultimately, the process of rightly viewing the any image I make and do is a process of forgetting "self", feeling beyond spatial and temporal "point of view", and (on that basis) freely and egolessly participating in That Which Is Prior to "point of view".

10.

There are two dimensions to Reality—the conditional, and the Non-conditional.

The image-art I make and do exhibits the two dimensions of Reality—and both of the dimensions of Reality are exhibited in the case of each and every image I make and do.

The two principal conditional aspects of the image-art I make and do are the perceived "subject" of the any image and the "point-of-view"-perceiver who looks at the image.

Reality Itself—or That Which Always Already Exists Prior to "point of view"—is the Non-conditional dimension of the image-art I make and do.

The viewer's right participation in the any image I make and do is not merely a matter of focusing "in" the any image for its own sake—or confining feeling-attention to the image, within and of itself (like a tapestry without a "weaver's exit"*).

* "Weaver's exit" is a reference to the Navajo tradition of the "weaver's pathway" or "spirit line"—an intentional line or break in the design of a rug or other weaving, understood as the means by which the weaver's spirit and creativity would escape entrapment in the woven pattern.

Any image (or even any thought or any perception), in and of itself, is merely a kind of maze, or a "room" without an exit, or a mode of entrapment in and by "point of view" (or ego's "I").

Rather than being an end in itself, the any image I make and do is an aesthetically fabricated means for participatory ecstasy—wherein and whereby the any rightly participating viewer tacitly transcends "point of view" (or the otherwise inescapable "room" of egoity) by means of participation in Reality Itself.

11.

The image-art I make and do is about entering (or transferring) into the Intrinsically egoless Transcendental Sphere and State of Reality Itself.

That process always begins in the sphere of conditionality and superficiality—with the "subjects" of moment to moment attention.

Fully participating in the image-art I make and do requires the viewer to deal with—and go beyond—the "subject-self" (or ego-"self", or "point-of-view-self").

Therefore, fullest right participation in the image-art I make and do is, itself, a profound form of "self"-discipline.

12.

Whatever people look at, they see a reflection of themselves.

Whatever people look at, they manifest themselves in response.

Whatever people look at, they show their own shape in response.

Whatever people look at, they feel their own shape in response.

Therefore, an intrinsic discipline of the habits of egoity—and of "point of view" itself—is required in order to rightly, fully, and fruitfully participate in the image-art I make and do.

XII.

The Secret of How To Know (and Be Known By) My Participatory Image-Art

The experience (and even the potential expression and utterance) that indicates right and true participation in the image-art I make and do is never merely "correct"—or a characterization of the only possible appropriate experience, and expression, and utterance relative to the image there—but it is (if truly right) intrinsically (or self-authentically) true to the viewer-participant.

Every image-form I make and do (including both flat-forms and sculptural forms) should be approached and experienced as a kind of living "presence"—to be embraced, and fully and freely participated in, and (altogether) combined with, in order to "know" and be "known" in the process.

In this manner of approach, the any image-form I make and do must be fully accepted as a living "presence" (or as a part of the viewing-participant's own living process), rather than as a mere "object", intrinsically and irreducibly separate from the viewer's body-mind-totality.

Every image-form I make and do should be (thus) approached and understood as an image-assisted "subjective" (or in-person) process, in and for—and, also, always intrinsically transcending—the any and every particular viewer who participates in it with whole bodily (or tacit and total psycho-physical) attention.

That image-assisted "subjective" process—which is (intrinsically, and in-person-intimately) a tacit (or intrinsically thought-transcending, and ego-transcending) process of "knowing" and being (in effect) "known" by the image-form I present to the participatory viewer—is (therefore) made fully evident only in any and every moment of fully right and true viewing-participation in it.

Therefore, the image-art I make and do is finally fabricated (or made fully experientially evident) only in the any and every moment of any viewer's right and true participation in it.

XIII.

My Non-Objective Art of Image

Reality Itself Is Intrinsically and Self-Evidently egoless, Non-separate, and Indivisible.

Therefore, all conditionally arising perception Is—As Is (or merely as it is, inherently prior to egoic, or separate and separative, "self"-consciousness)—the Self-Consciousness of Reality Itself.

All ego-based (or egoically "self"-conscious) "knowledge" is mere ideas—inherently "self"-separated (or "self"-contracted) from the Self-Consciousness of Reality Itself.

Reality Itself Is the egoless, Non-separate, and Indivisible Pre-Context of all mere (or pre-mental, and thought-free) perception.

Mere (or pre-mental, and thought-free) perception Is an inherently sacred (or boundlessly deep and profound)—but, also, in and of itself, non-religious—event of Reality-participation.

All mere perception Is egoless participation in the Self-Condition of Reality Itself—Inherently (and, Thus, Perfectly) Prior to all acts of "self"-contraction (or of separate-"self"-presumption and separate-"object"-causation).

All thinking, all mere ideas, all seeking for "knowledge" of "objects", and all "knowing" of "objects" is (and, indeed, all "objects" themselves are) egoic non-participation in the Self-Condition of Reality Itself.

Mere perception Is Intrinsic Self-Apperception—or Intrinsic Self-Recognition—of the Self-Nature, Self-Condition, and Self-State of Reality Itself.

To merely perceive—and, thus, to Priorly, Inherently, Intrinsically, Non-separately, and egolessly Self-Recognize—what otherwise appears as "objective" (or as an "object", whether "internal" or "external") Is to Self-Awaken the Intrinsic Self-Consciousness of Reality Itself.

Tacit (and, thus, intrinsically egoless) participatory mere perception of any and all conditionally arising appearances Inherently (and, Thus, Perfectly) Coincides with the Tacit Intrinsic Self-Apperception (or Self-Apprehension) of the Intrinsically egoless Self-Consciousness of Reality Itself.

Therefore, most fully right and true art-forms coincide with the artist's egoless Coincidence with the state of mere perception and (thus, and most fundamentally) with the Intrinsically Self-Evident

State of the Self-Apperception, Self-Apprehension, or Inherent Self-Consciousness of Reality Itself.

All most fully right and true art (and, thus, every most fully right and true art-form) serves to assist any and every would-be perceiver to participate in the egoless state of Coincidence with mere perception—and, in that event, with the therein Self-Evident State of the Self-Apperception, Self-Apprehension, or Inherent Self-Consciousness of Reality Itself.

My art of image is, in the active doing, always (Inherently) conformed to the Intrinsically Self-Evident event of Intrinsically egoless participatory Coincidence with mere perception—and, Thus, with the Intrinsically Self-Evident State of the Self-Apperception, Self-Apprehension, or Inherent Self-Consciousness of Reality Itself, Intrinsically Self-Recognizing all of the merely apparent "objective" all.

My art of image is—Thus, and As Such—always (Inherently) purposed to serve and assist the Great Event of Reality-Coincidence in one and all who would perceive As Is.

XIV.

Perfect Abstraction

1.

Any and every apparently three-dimensional form of visual experience is—in the immediate instant of any apparent moment of specific experiential observation—intrinsically and self-evidently a two-dimensional (or flat-field) mode of image-experience.

In any specific observational instant, the visual phenomenon is, intrinsically and self-evidently, a timeless, non-changing, flat-field appearance of juxtaposed elements (such as colors, shapes, and lines), and (altogether) a depthless flat space (or image) of mutually opposing or (otherwise) mutually supportive visual signs (or observables).

No matter how intensively (or for how long a period of time) anyone may walk around or within an apparently three-dimensional form, that walk-around or walk-within is—in the immediate instant of any apparent moment of visual observation in the walking-time of the process—a moment of mere image (or flat-field experience).

Mere image is intrinsically egoless, flat-patterned, non-familiar, abstract, and unique.

Mere image is never totally comprehensive, or inclusive of all possible views in space, time, or space-time.

Every mere-image instant points beyond itself to an existential totality that cannot be comprehensively and finally experienced or "known".

Likewise, every mere-image instant points beyond itself to the egoless, Indivisible, all-and-All-Inclusive, and all-and-All-Transcending Self-Nature, Self-Condition, and Self-State That Is Reality Itself.

2.

All perception is abstraction.

All that is experienced by or from a "point of view" in space, or time, or space-time is non-totality, a selection, a partial view, a mere fraction of the whole.

Every perception experienced by or from a "point of view" is an egoic (or "self"-referring) fabrication.

Right and true visual art (or image-art) must render the "point-of-view"-made and intrinsically ego-bound fabrications that comprise ordinary perception back to the whole of totality.

Right and true visual art (or image-art) must render the "point-of-view"-made and intrinsically ego-bound abstractions that comprise ordinary perception back to the egoless Reality-Source in which perception is otherwise ego-bound.

Right and true visual art (or image-art) is the ego-transcending process of Perfect Abstraction.

XV.

The Unobservable Totality of Light

My image-art can be characterized as paradoxical space that undermines "point of view". That undermining (which occurs in the any instant of fully felt participation in any of the images I make and show) allows for a tacit glimpse, or intuitive sense, of the Transcendental Condition of Reality (even as all conditional appearances, and, Ultimately, As It Is)—always, inherently, and totally beyond and prior to "point of view".

The human individual in the midst of perceived reality is like a camera in a room—perceiving everything from a fixed "point of view". Any one and every one in a room separately perceives the whatever they think and feel they see—but what does the room (itself) really look like? What is the appearance of the room itself—as a totality, as a whole, and As it Is? The room (itself) is an always unobserved (and Perfectly Unobservable) totality—a seamless, simultaneous, and non-separate whole, indivisibly conjoined (in Prior Unity) with the all-and-All of time, and space, and light, and all the All of Prior's Depth, and all the All of All Reality Itself. The room (itself), like even the universe as a whole, exists only As it Is, inherently prior to every "point of view" (or ego-"I"), and always (irreducibly) as it would appear when viewed from every possible "point of view" in space-time—not merely as it would appear from any one and particular "point of view" (or separate ego-"I"), or from even any finite collection of the seeming selves of "points of view".

No particular "point of view" can reveal the "room" itself, or the universe itself, or Reality Itself—because every "point of view" is inherently limited and intrinsically "self"-referring.

Reality Itself always already exists. Reality Itself Is the One, and Only, and All, and What That Exists—always Prior to "point of view", and always before any individual "point of view" constructs its version of separately "self"-presumed "reality".

"Point of view" is the essence of ego-life: The apparently individual being presumes that he or she is a particularized "point", or a psycho-physically self-organized "point of view", in space-time. And that "point" is "made" by contracting from the always prior and indivisible (and intrinsically egoless) condition of totality—and, indeed, by contracting from even every mode, form, or state of conditional existence that is not "local" (or even identical) to the "point of view" (or ego-"I") of "self"-reference. Nevertheless, the "room" itself (As Is) exists always already non-"locally" (or comprehensively, inclusive of innumerable potential "locations" of "point of view")—and, as that totality, the "room" itself exists inherently prior to all possible "points of view", and such that the "room" itself is (inherently, and paradoxically) un-"locatable" and unobservable.

My images are always artistic demonstrations of the Non-conditional and Inherently Un-observable (and, thus, Transcendental) Reality-Condition of whatever is (apparently) perceived—and (simultaneously) they are also root-"imagings" of the conditional (or naturally perceived) states and appearances of the psycho-physically constructed phenomena of "ordinary" human experience. My process of image-art is always purposed to transcend "point of view"—and, if the resultant images are received seriously and viewed seriously, they are, for the any and every such viewer, a means for tacitly feeling the Transcendental, irreducibly paradoxical, and intrinsically incomprehensible Real, and Indivisible, and all-Simultaneous, and Non-separate, and Perfectly egoless Condition of that which is (presently) conditionally perceived (and, thus and thereby, presumed to be "reality"). The Reality-Condition of all that appears to arise conditionally Is Perfectly Non-conditional and Intrinsically egoless (or Irreducibly Prior to "point of view"). Indeed, even the human body-mind-"self" (or "self"-presumed separate ego-"I") is intrinsically egoless (or Inherently Prior to the presumption of "location", separateness, or any reduction to a "point" in space and time)—for even the body extends into such enough of space that no finite "point" in space can be said to be its "location".

My image-art is always "in" the "space" of the irreducible Reality-Condition of all that is conditionally and naturally perceived and "known". Thus, by making image-art, I am making "space" for What Is Beyond and Prior to "point of view" and ego-"I".

My process of creating images brings together two principal elements, in a complex approach. One is the comprehensive element of form, and the other is the element of fundamental content (or essential meaning). On the one hand, I constantly exercise the formal element, and, thus and so (and by means of an always spontaneously free process of improvisation), I strictly control and order the structure of the images I invent. On the other hand, I am (likewise constantly) intent upon maintaining and profoundly enlarging the characteristic of meaning. Indeed, the meaning-content is always primary. The meaning-context (rather than the formal context in and of itself) is always the "subject" to which I respond by making the any image I make. Therefore, the work I do with the formal aspects of an image must (I insist) always responsively coincide with the preservation and enlargement of the fundamental context of meaning—no matter how much of an abstraction the image may become in the formal process of improvisational invention. Consequently, the tension between meaning and form is fundamental to all the image-making work I do.

The idea (expressed by Cézanne, and by various other artists and artistic movements since the time of Cézanne) that artistically fashioned visual form is to be based on primary geometric elements has also been fundamental to the artistic training and familiarity I have developed with art, from the time I was a boy. Indeed, if the deep process whereby the brain makes perception happen is profoundly felt and (thus) understood, then it can also be understood that the basis of the natural world's construction as perceptual experience is primary geometry, or elemental shape—curved, linear, and angular. Everything perceived is a structure that demonstrates the interaction of these three all-patterning forces of shape. The intrinsically unobservable (and, thus, unknowably complex) intersection of circles, squares, and triangles (or of curved, linear, and angular geometric, or geometrically-organizing, forces) makes (or structures and organizes) virtually every perceptible natural shape.

The natural world itself is (inherently) a self-morphing and self-limiting construction (or a naturally improvised and spontaneously self-organizing art-form), formalized and fabricated by means of a plastic interaction between primary forces and structures—but the natural world is so complex in its combinations of root-forces of shaping-energy (and, thus, of primary geometries) that (except in some generalized and, generally, non-specific sense) the primaries are, characteristically, not perceived by any natural perceiver. However, it is altogether possible to tacitly feel that whatever is actually being perceived in any moment is something structured in the primary geometric manner, and that (consequently) all apparent complexity is based on very simple primary elements. My image-art is (on this basis) a demonstration (by spontaneously responsive formal artistic means) of the naturally perceived world (or any naturally perceived "subject", or meaning-context) as multiples of primary geometries—always (in every instant of conjunction) intersecting with each other (often numerously, or even uncountably), such that the naturally perceptible resultant form is (itself) a unique and discretely perceptible structure of "meaningful form", wherein the root-geometries may (or may not) remain (themselves) discernible.

My image-art is not (in any instance) merely a "something" in and of itself, or an "objective something" that has, in the conventional sense, "subjective" meaning that only I can understand or know. My images are about how Reality Is (in and of and As Itself), and, also, how Reality appears (as a construction made of primary shaping-forces) in the context of natural perception. My image-art is, therefore, not merely "subjectively" (or, otherwise, "objectively") based—but, rather, the images I make and do always tacitly and utterly coincide with Reality As It Is (Itself, and altogether). Therefore, I have called the process of the image-art I make and do "Transcendental Realism".

Reality (Itself, and, also, in the context of conditional, or perceptual, appearances) has (inherently, or As It Is) no "thing" in it, no "other" in it, no separate "self" in it, no ideas, no constructs in mind or perception, and (altogether) no "point of view". The irreducible paradox of unobservability and unknowability is the actual (Real) state of every one and every thing—even in the apparent context of all things arising.

The living body inherently wants to Realize (or Be One With) the Matrix of life. The living body always wants (with wanting need) to allow the Light of Perfect Reality into the "room". Assisting human beings to fulfill that impulse is what I work to do by every act of image-art. My images are created to be a means for any and every perceiving, feeling, and fully participating viewer to "Locate" Fundamental and Really Perfect Light—the world As Light, all relations As Light, conditional (or naturally perceived) light As Absolute Light.

My images, well-met, should bring tears to the eyes, restore laughter to the life, and (altogether) both show and give a perfect equanimity to the total world.

The "room" is how and where the construction (or always illusory and temporary fabrication) of ego-"I" (or "point of view") and even all "locality" happens. Ultimately, when "point of view" is transcended, there is no longer any "room" (or any separate "location" and separate "self") at all—but only Love-Bliss-"Brightness", limitlessly felt, in vast unpatterned Joy.

XVI.

The Visual Realization of Insecurity and Truth

Adi Da Samraj working on *The Goddess of New York*,
with the three-screen setup he characteristically used in his art studio.

1.

In the image-art I make and do, there are many levels of meaning. The perceived meaning will, in each case, depend on what the viewer brings to it altogether—and any individual will bring something different each time he or she looks at the images.

Therefore, the images are not static. You cannot "get" any of the images I make and do merely by giving it a glance. You must participate in the image. That participation is a process, and it has no finality, no end point. The meaning of any image cannot be conclusively defined. No verbal explanation can encompass the entirety of any image's meaning.

Viewing the image-art I make and do is always a process. Thus, viewing the image-art I make and do is not about coming to an end-point. The complexity and the multi-level nature of the images I make and do is such that your viewing of any given image cannot ever be conclusively "finished".

My image-art is not an "answer".

My image-art is not a "question".

My image-art does not have a beginning.

My image-art does not have an ending.

You cannot "get"—or encompass, or control—the image-art I make and do.

That is why, as a general rule, I make image-art in monumental scale. You cannot control an image that is larger than your own body. Dealing with any of the monumental images I make and do is a process—a process in which you must participate, a process to which you must be given over. You cannot ever bring that process to an end. You cannot finalize that process. You cannot ever "put the image to rest" by "putting it into words".

There are all kinds of things a person might say in any given moment of response to the image-art I make and do, but such remarks simply are a matter of the reflective verbalizing that can occur in the midst of the process of non-verbally participating in the image-art.

The image always transcends you. Such is the nature of the image-art I make and do.

2.

The figurative images I make and do are no more "comprehensible" than the most abstract images I make and do. The figurative images are not merely representational references. Simply because they contain representational elements does not make the figurative images actually recognizable and representational.

My use of forms is such that they are always equally abstract—whether they appear to be representational (or to have some likeness to conventional perceptual experience) or not. It makes no difference whether an image appears to be figurative or abstract—in neither case can you "say what it is" with complete finality. You can only participate in any of the images I make and do each time you bring yourself to look at one of them. You cannot summarize the any image in a final verbal accounting.

In the ego-mind, there is a will to control things. The ego-mind wants to "get it", "say it", have it under control, and dissociate from it. My image-art is intended not to allow such control and dissociation. My image-art is intended to be "too big", in every respect, to allow such control and dissociation. My image-art is intended to have such force—both of form and of meaning, and even of physical size—that the images cannot be "grasped", or controlled, by the viewer. In the moment of participating in the image-art I make and do, the egoic will to control and dissociate cannot be finally exercised. My image-art is specifically intended to confound that impulse.

When people ask questions—about art, or about anything else—they are really expressing a feeling of being confounded. They want an answer in order to get control of whatever is confounding them—so that they can then dissociate from what is confounding them. The impulse is to "get the knowledge" in order to get whatever is confounding under control. That is a fundamental impulse of human beings—particularly in the current era of human time. Such is the characteristic attitude of scientific materialism. However, nothing about the world can actually be "gotten under control". You can presume that you have something under control, by virtue of your "knowledge" about it—but that is an illusion.

In the words of a traditional saying, "This maya cannot be comprehended"—or, in other words, "Nothing that arises as world or experience can be contained by human understanding." That is a fact—it cannot. Indeed, Reality Itself cannot be comprehended, contained, and controlled. However, at the present time, humankind is thoroughly bound up in the illusion that it can (and must) comprehend (or contain) this appearance, that it can "know" this appearance, and (thereby) get control over this appearance.

The ego-"I" presumes that, by means of "knowledge", it can protect itself from what it is perceiving. To the ego-"I", the world is a totality that is overwhelming. The pursuit of "knowledge", in order to get the world under control, is fundamental to the ego-effort in which human beings are now concentrated. However, the possibility of such control is an illusion.

My image-suite entitled *The Goddess of New York* exemplifies the human situation relative to the intrinsic failure of human "knowledge" to grant the "knower" the ability to contain and control the events of experience. *The Goddess of New York* is about a "knowledge" that cannot be spoken about, a "knowledge" that makes one silent. New York has not figured anything out. It is not even talking what it "knows". New York—and even the total human world—is stuck with something that it does not know what to do with. It is "knowledge" as shock. Thus, *The Goddess of New York* is about 9/11—and everything else. Indeed, the "subject" of *The Goddess of New York* is everything that is not the "Perfect Knowledge" of Reality Itself. At the same time, *The Goddess of New York* cannot be confined to any particular meaning or set of meanings. All different kinds of meanings are there. Whatever sensibility a person brings to the images in any moment, or allows himself or herself to feel by participating in the images, that is what the meaning is for that individual in that moment.

The event of 9/11 is about the failure of the myth of "knowledge", the myth that human beings can "know" and control. The image of the mouth in *The Goddess of New York* is about disillusionment with "knowing". You have not figured it out. But it is not only that you will not figure it out—you cannot figure it out. That is the Nature of Reality Itself. You can be given over to Reality

Itself, surrendered into Reality Itself, and Reality Itself can be Realized—but you cannot figure out Reality Itself, in the sense of "knowing" Reality Itself "objectively" and (thereby) getting control over Reality Itself.

That morning of 9/11, people in New York "had their act together". As far as they were concerned, everything was "under control", and they were "on top of it". A couple of hours later, they had the look on their faces that is seen in *The Goddess of New York*. And it is a permanent look. The expression on that mouth is not going to go away. It is the primal human expression of illusions having been destroyed, such that you can no longer persist on the basis of the illusion of "knowing" and controlling.

You cannot control a Goddess. The iconic figure of the Goddess is about something that controls <u>you</u>, something that you cannot control, something that is not comprehensible—something that has not the slightest sympathy with your egoic will to "know" and control.

Being fixed in that infinite paradox is the actual nature of the human situation—not the illusion of "knowing" and "being on top of it". However, that illusion of "knowing" is a fundamental part of the "self"-image of human beings in the present epoch, as epitomized, perhaps, by New Yorkers—the illusion that, in the end, humankind will have everything "under control" through "knowledge".

Goddesses require surrender. You cannot know a Goddess the way a man may know his girlfriend. The woman-form in *The Goddess of New York* is not amenable to that kind of disposition. Nevertheless, the woman-form in *The Goddess of New York* also displays the human characteristic of sympathy, the human force of being confounded and having no "answers", the human situation of struggling in the midst of anguish and anger.

The shock of 9/11 is about the loss of the illusion of power, and confrontation with a power that you cannot control and cannot understand. However, *The Goddess of New York* is also about everything altogether—not only about the 9/11 event.

Something powerful struck those twin towers—and, in general, nobody knows what it is about. Being alive is exactly like that.

You are standing firm, as if you are in control—as if you are going to live forever, and be master of the world, or at least of your own life. All of that is an illusion. In actuality, life is a shocking experience—and it never stops being that, until there is perfect transcendence.

The illusion of "answers" is just that—an illusion. Realization of Reality Itself is not an "answer" to a "question". Reality Itself transcends the "question", the "answer", the "questioner", the dilemma—because Reality Itself is about transcending the ego-"I" and the shock of conditional experience.

The 9/11 event is a kind of mythological happening—in the sense that it totally confounds the "knower" of it. As such, 9/11 has become a universal symbol for the shock of being alive—which includes the shock of "knowing" about death and, at the same time, not "knowing" about it.

Not being able to be in control is shocking, disturbing, and requires a struggle. If you really accept that you are not in control, you should be moved or stimulated to enter into a process that has to do with the most fundamental dilemma of your own existence.

A Goddess is a myth about Reality and experience. A Goddess is a personification. Any experience can be said to personify Reality altogether. Therefore, every experience is a kind of a myth. Every experience has mythic force. The degree of that force depends on how profound you are willing to be.

All of this is fundamental to what the images I make and do are about. My images are made in order to enable people to enter into the most serious of matters.

What is the benefit of participation in the image-art I make and do? There is the "aesthetic experience", in the sense of appreciating and enjoying the formal values of the images—but, otherwise, participation in the image-art I make and do is about entering into the profundity of the essentially unanswerable context of human life.

That does not mean that human existence is nothing but a puzzle, that there is no way beyond the unanswered state, that the situation of not having anything under control and not "knowing" anything is the "last word" on the matter. My image-art is not merely about that kind of existential dead end. My image-art is also about the Realization of Reality Itself—and that Realization requires one to go beyond the struggle of human existence, and beyond egoity altogether.

Each of the images I make and do is intended to function as a context for that kind of profoundly serious process. At the same time, the image-art I make and do can also be enjoyed simply in terms of its aesthetic characteristics. The formal characteristics, the structures, the colors, the relationship of forms to one another, and so forth, can be enjoyed in their own right—without involving oneself in consideration of the fundamental context and dilemma of existence. But the image-art I make and do can also be entered into in the most profound manner.

3.

Everything potentially "looks like" something—to whoever looks at it. You can look into the clouds in the sky and see faces, or whatever. Any visual shape can be felt to have some kind of recognizability. Therefore, even the Geome and Linead forms I make and do can suggest modes of perceptual experience or conceptual experience—through their shapes, arrangements, colors, and so forth. Nevertheless, the fundamental essence of the image-art I make and do is not involved with recognizability-reference.

The root of perception is a flux without conventional recognizability. "Point of view" is what "causes" recognizability. If "point of view" is suspended or transcended, there is not anything that is recognizable, familiar, or comprehensible.

Therefore, the fact that, in a suite such as *The Goddess of New York*, there are figurative forms does not mean that those forms are essentially recognizable. If the forms seem recognizable, it is only because "point of view" is being assumed. If "point of view" is not assumed, then the images are not recognizable—even where there are apparent recognizability-references to female figure, airplane, or whatever it may be.

In the transcending of "point of view", all recognizability vanishes. Nothing is recognizably structured in space-time, apart from "point of view". Apart from "point of view", what does a room look like? If one cannot even comprehend a room apart from taking up a position, or "point of view", within it, how does one expect to comprehend the universe?

Therefore, the transcending of "point of view", or the intrinsic egolessness of human experience, is fundamental to the image-art I make and do. The viewer may feel attached to "point of view" and interpret the images with reference to "point of view". That is what people do—moment to moment—in ordinary life. Things seem recognizable only with reference to "point of view"—or ego-"I".

In fact, Reality Itself is egoless. It is not that egolessness can be attained, and, then, all of a sudden, the room vanishes. Rather, even if there is apparent perception from a position of apparent space-time-"locatedness", the event is egoless, and nothing is recognizable—nothing, no one. Whether or not things appear in a conventionally recognizable manner (or, at least, in a manner that is, in some terms, recognizable) makes no difference. Whether anything arises or does not arise, it is the same situation: In Reality Itself, "point of view" is inherently illusory, or Really non-existing.

In the "point-of-view"-position, the ego-mind wants to "know" and control. The ego-mind wants to fix things with reference to "point of view". However, Reality Itself will not allow that to occur. The "Goddess of New York" will not allow that to occur. And the totality of events in New York will not allow that to occur. In fact, there is not anything that allows that to occur. That things could ever be fixed in reference to "point of view" is an illusion, a futile search.

The search to be in control, and immune in ego's "point of view", is intrinsically futile. The individual is inherently confronted by what transcends the ego-"self", or "point of view". What intrinsically transcends the ego-"I" inherently demands absolute surrender—not surrender in the conventional sense of "enslavement", but surrender in the sense of relinquishing the presumption and illusory security of "locatedness", or the "point of view" as different (or intrinsically dissociated) from all other positions and identities, defending itself with reference to everything and everyone, and trying to survive through the "self"-defense of that struggle.

Such is the paradox in *The Goddess of New York*. The confounding of the search is fundamental to its force of meaning.

4.

Image-art is a visually-based process, not a word-based process. Therefore, image-art bypasses the word-based mind. People want to talk about image-art and explain it—but, at last, all of that is a means of dissociating from the image-process.

The image-process is inherently wordless. Words in association with the force of sheer visual experience are paradoxical. The words themselves become nothing but shapes. There is no explanation.

The visual process is its own domain of process altogether. The visual (or right-brained) process is, intrinsically, without reference to the left-brained mode of the human scale of doings, which is the verbal (or thinking) mind.

That is part of the virtue of visual art. Part of the potential of visual art is that it can draw people into a process that bypasses the verbal mind and deals with great profundities—if people will enter into it profoundly, completely apart from any kind of talk whatsoever. Rightly entered into, visual art is another place, an oasis away from talk. It is a different mode of thinking than verbal thinking. It is perceptual thinking—and, ultimately, it is a mode of non-thinking, or of direct apprehension.

Nevertheless, the visual process of right and true image-art is not merely a matter of "staring into space"—or, like a zombie, staring at the wallpaper, with a vaporous glee behind the eyes. The visual process of right and true image-art is not a demented kind of non-thinking. Rather, the visual process of right and true image-art is a different mode of intelligently apprehending Reality than the verbal process.

In daily life, people confront one another with a mixture of all different kinds of perceptual and conceptual happenings, all at once—as if the manner in which you look at things and the manner in which you talk about things are the same event. In actuality, perceptual activity and conceptual activity are different worlds, different modes of participation in conditional experience—and the two do not directly have anything to do with one another—just as mind has nothing intrinsically to do with the body. The body is usually associated with the mind, and with conventions of thinking—but, essentially, a discipline is required to bring the mind into full coincidence with the body.

Of course, visual processes that are called "art" do not necessarily have to be profound. How much visual art is even intended to be profound? Much visual art is as superficial as a conversation on a street corner—and even intentionally so. Visual art done in that manner relinquishes its potential for profundity and for drawing people into participation in profundity—even the intrinsically ego-transcending profundity of Reality Itself. In the case of truly profound visual art, the fundamental right and true process happens in a domain of participation that is intensely and deeply non-verbal.

Of course, visual art is often used to enforce or perpetuate states of mind and presumption that are governed through verbal-mind messages. A lot of art propagandizes a verbal-mind-based presumption about life. Such propagandizing is a limit on the profundity of art. To associate art with religious or political or any other form of propaganda places a limit on what art can do. Similarly, the "post-modern" stance that "there is no difference between art and reality" places a limit on what art can do.

Art has the potential to draw the participant into profundity—beyond talk, and beyond the controls that the verbal mind imposes on awareness. I intend the image-art I make and do to go beyond a whole mass of limitations that are commonly presumed to be what visual art is for and what it is about.

Therefore, the image-art I make and do works in a domain of profundity that is not typically exercised in the domain of visual art. Typically, a limit is—by either "official" or "personal" means—set on the degree of profundity that will be "allowed". That limit is set by verbal mind, ego-"I", nationalist sentiments, religious propaganda, all kinds of things—conventional "isms" of one or another kind, whatever they may be. All such limits are merely means of perpetuating an already-entrenched presumption of limitation and illusion.

The image-art I make and do is (specifically, and intentionally) about not having any such presumptions, and (thereby) going beyond all such limits. I put no limits on the meaning-force and profundity people could enter into if they seriously approach the image-art I make and do. The image-art I make and do is for the purpose of enabling people to enter into the greatest profundity that image-art can serve.

When I make images, by whatever means (whether digital or photographic or by hand), I am (in that very process) actively transcending the limitations of the "point-of-view"-machine that is the human ego-"I". However, by making images, I am also looking to enable the viewer to be moved beyond the presumption of space-time-"locatedness", to be moved beyond the propagandized verbal mind that binds human beings, and to be moved out of the fixed-minded regime of ego-bondage in which human beings characteristically live.

Fundamentally, all of the images I make and do are Self-Portraits of Reality Itself, the Reality-Condition Which is egoless (or "point-of-view"-less). To rightly and truly participate in any of the images I have made and done is to participate in Reality Itself. In order to participate in Reality Itself, "point of view" (or ego-"I") must be transcended—and, therefore, the illusion of separate "self" and all of its effort to "know", to control, to dissociate, to size everything down must be transcended. The effort to protect oneself from what is being experienced is confounded by right and true and full participation in the image-art I make and do.

I look to make images that are without limitations on profundity. I look to make image-art as profoundly as visual art can be made, and (thus) to enable the viewer to benefit from the most profound possibility of participation—without being limited by any presumptions or thinking or beliefs that people may otherwise have about art, or life, or the Nature of Reality Itself.

My image-art is rightly understood to be spiritual art—but it is not religious art, in the sense of serving the conventional purposes of institutionalized religion. The process of the image-art I make and do is non-religious, or even pre-religious.

The image-art I make and do is not fixed and limited by "point of view", or by even any mode of mentality, or by any mode of "self"-imagery that anyone might bring to the viewing of (and participating in) the image itself and the egoless Reality the image reveals to and via the sight.

Image-Art by Adi Da Samraj

The Pastimes of Narcissus, IV/1
(from *Spectra One*), 2006

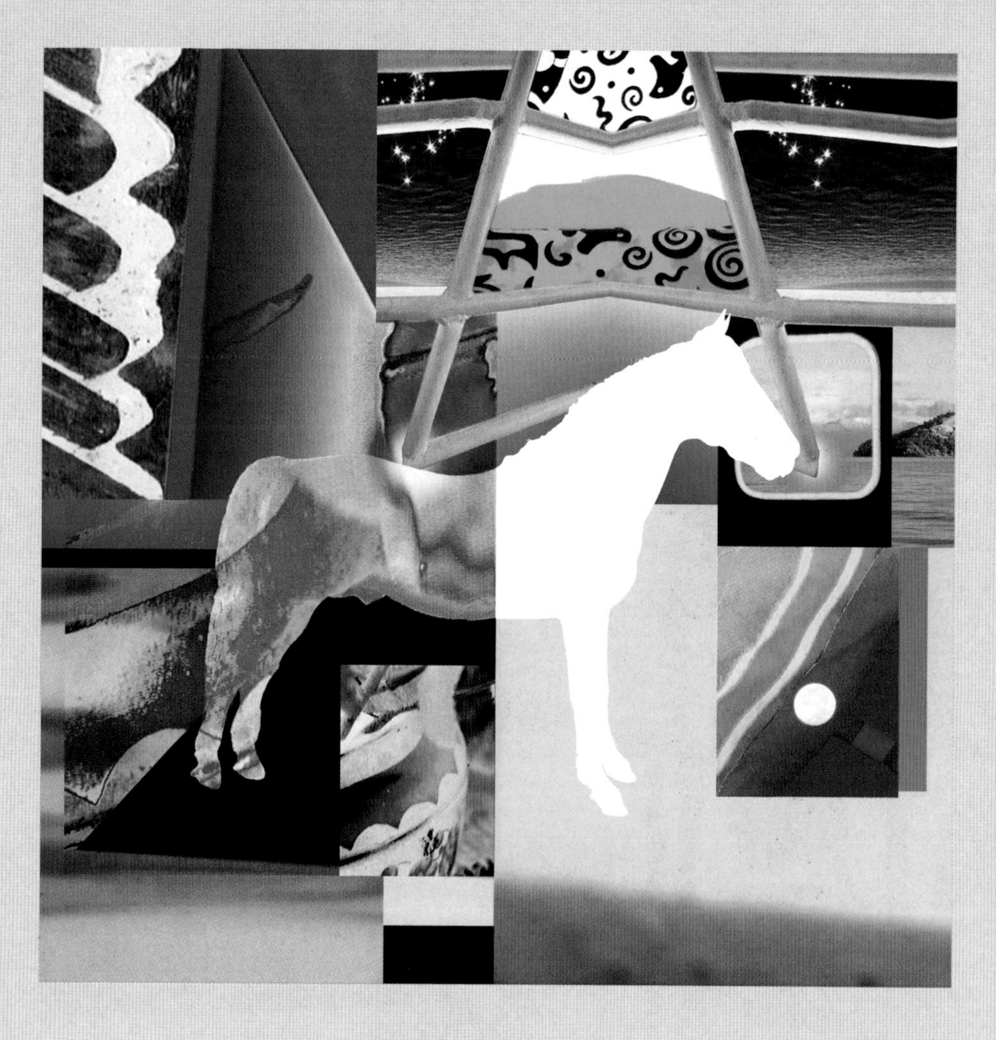

A Horse Appears In The Wild
Is Always Already The Case,
Part II: He/One 1
(from *Spectra Two*), 2006

A Horse Appears In The Wild
Is Always Already The Case,
Part III: She/One 1
(from *Spectra Two*), 2006

The Room Itself *Is* *The Only Witness To The Three Common States, V/8*
(from *Spectra Four*), 2006, 2007

The Autobiography Of Everybody,
Part II: The "He", The Single 2
(from *Spectra Nine*), 2006

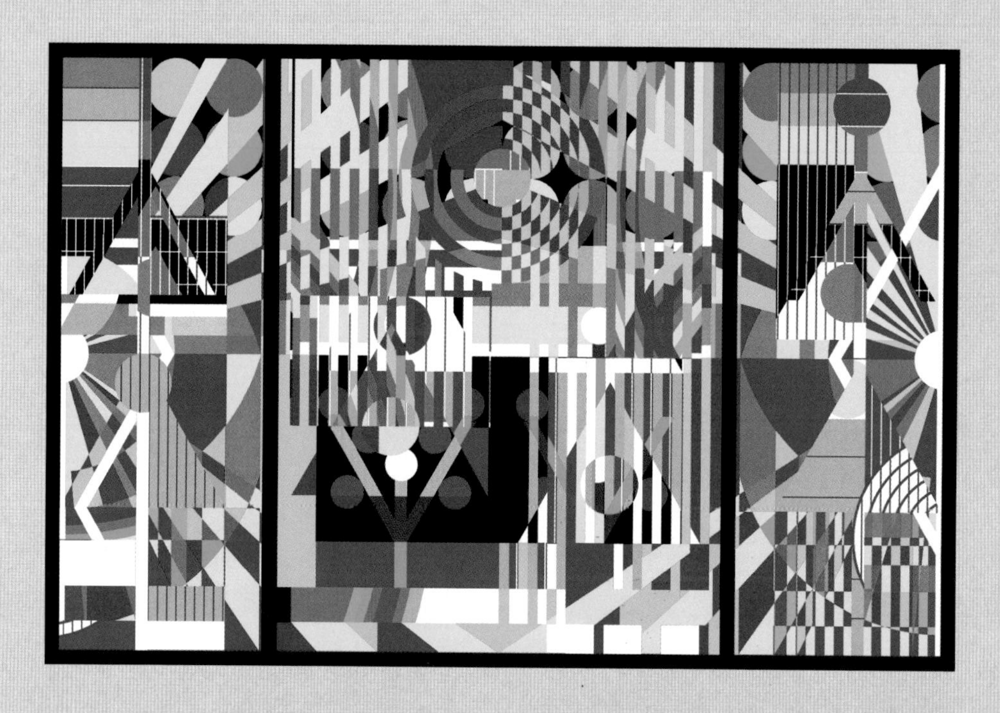

Alberti's Window, The Order Of The Day: Tuesday 8 (from *Geome One*), 2006

Alberti's Window, The Order Of The Day: Wednesday 8 (from *Geome One*), 2006

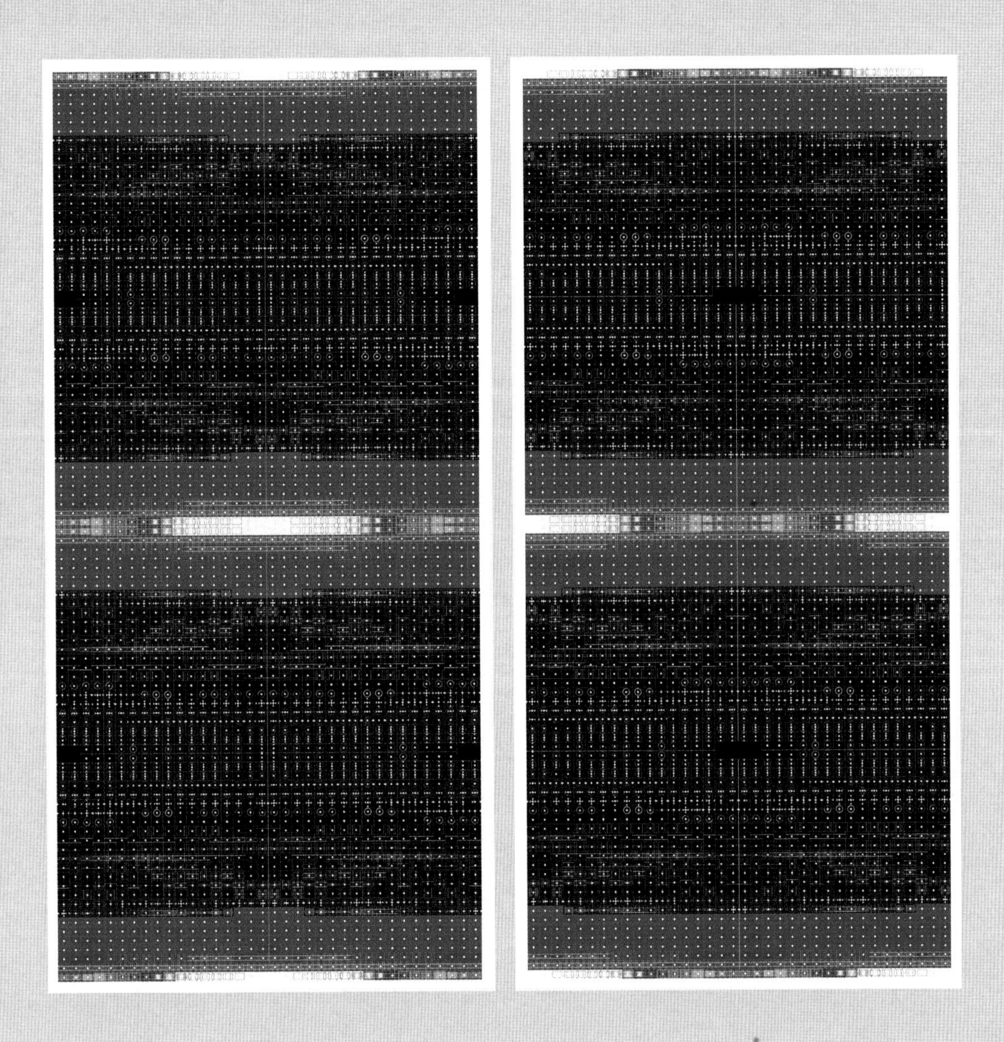

2001,
Part I: The Twin Towers, 2
(from *Geome Two*), 2006

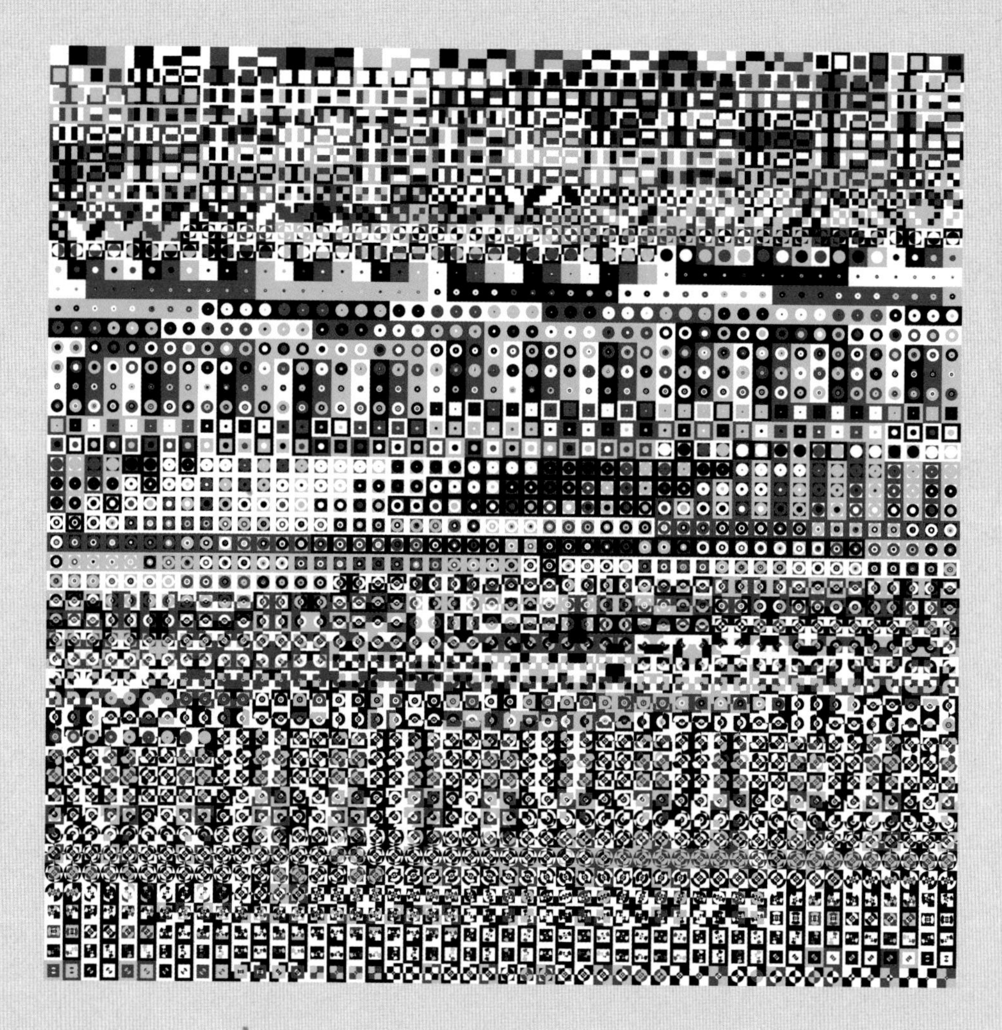

The Scale of Perfection,
Part One: NYC,
NYCSTET I
(from *Geome Three*), 2006

The Subject In Question,
He (The Naked State Of The Transcendental Subject) 10
(from *Geome Four*), 2006

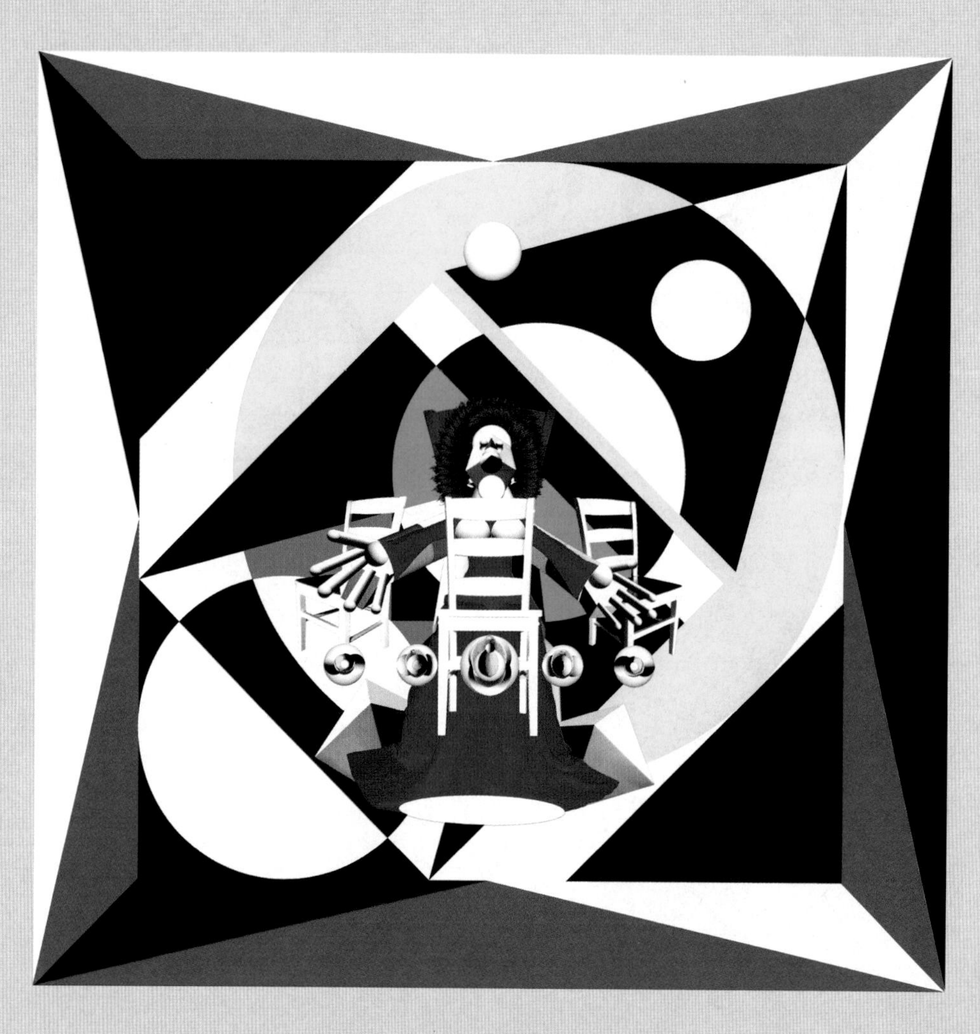

The Reduction Of The Beloved:
The Reduction Of The Beloved To Love Alone
(The Lover, The Bride, The Wife, The Widow)—
The Lover I
(from *Oculus One*), 2006, 2007

The Reduction Of The Beloved:
The Reduction Of The Beloved To As Is
(The Lover, The Bride, The Wife, The Widow)—
Part Five: The Widow, 3
(from *Oculus One*), 2006

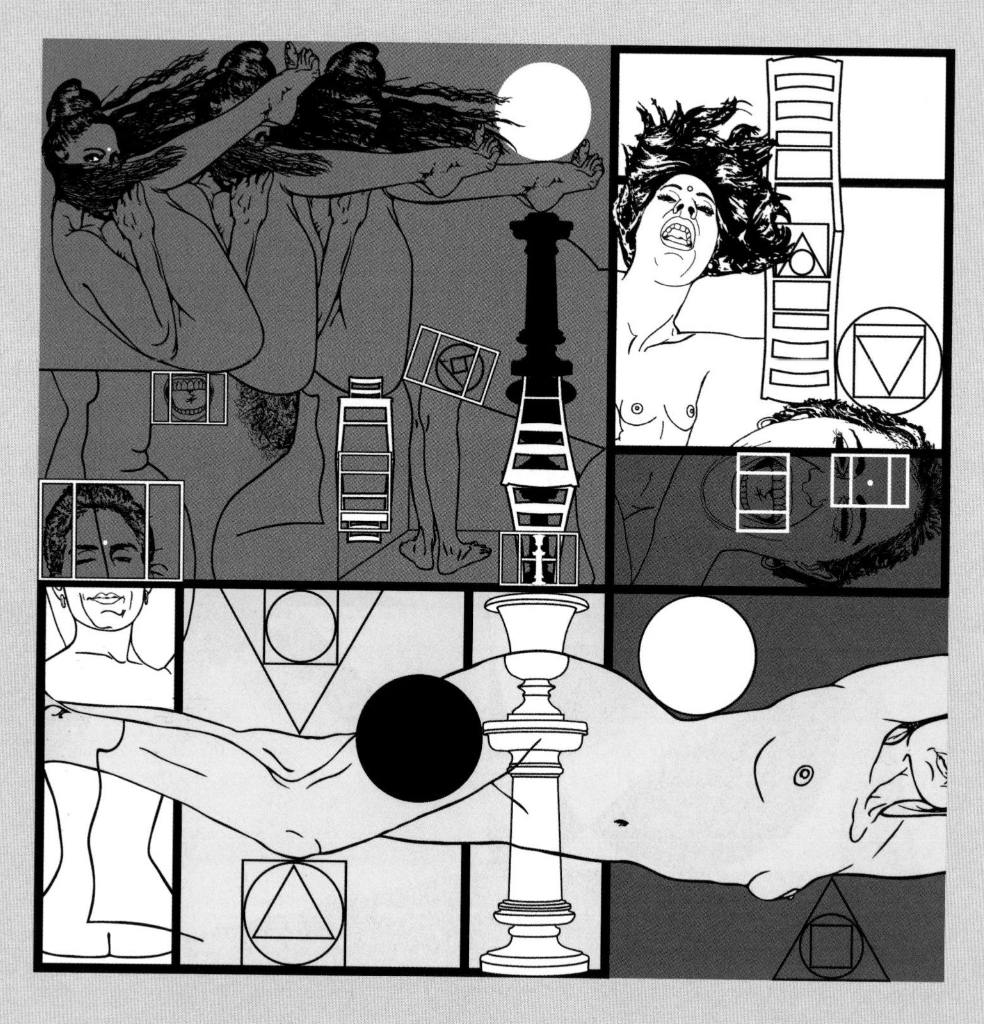

Alberti's Room,
Part Ten: Planes Quad Janes—Set 1, II
(from *Oculus Two*), 2006–2007

Alberti's Room,
Part Ten: Planes Quad Janes—Set 8, XI
(from *Oculus Two*), 2006–2007

The Spiritual Descent of The Bicycle Becomes The Second-Birth of Flight: Part Six – II
(from *Orpheus One*), 2007

The Spiritual Descent of The Bicycle Becomes The Second-Birth of Flight: Part Six – VII
(from *Orpheus One*), 2007

The Spiritual Descent of The Bicycle Becomes The Second-Birth of Flight: Part Eleven – VIII (from *Orpheus One*), 2007, 2008

Eurydice One: The Illusory Fall of The Bicycle
Into The Sub-Atomic Parallel Worlds of Primary Color and Point of View—
Part One: The Abstract Narrative In Geome, Linead, and Natural View – II/3
(from *Linead One*), 2007

Eurydice One: The Illusory Fall of The Bicycle
Into The Sub-Atomic Parallel Worlds of Primary Color and Point of View—
Part Two: The Abstract Narrative In Geome and Linead (First Stage) – II/1
(from *Linead One*), 2007

Eurydice One: The Illusory Fall of The Bicycle
Into The Sub-Atomic Parallel Worlds of Primary Color and Point of View—
Part Three: The Abstract Narrative In Geome and Linead (Second Stage) – I/2, second panel
(from *Linead One*), 2007, 2008

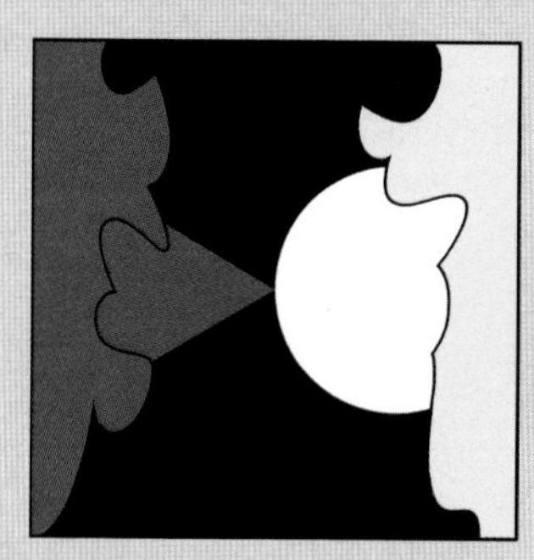

The Goddess of New York:
Part One – VIII/16, 2007

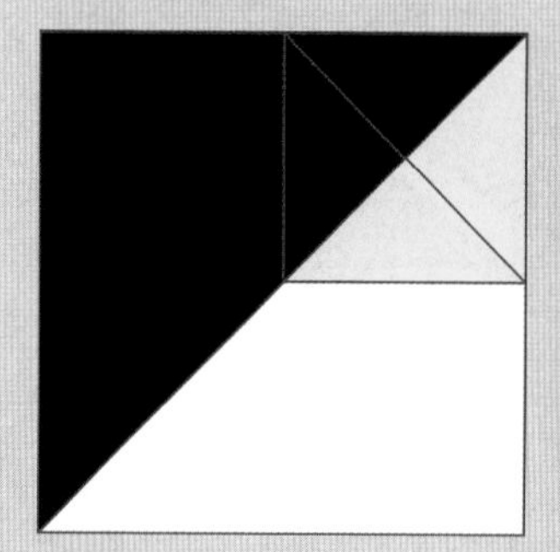
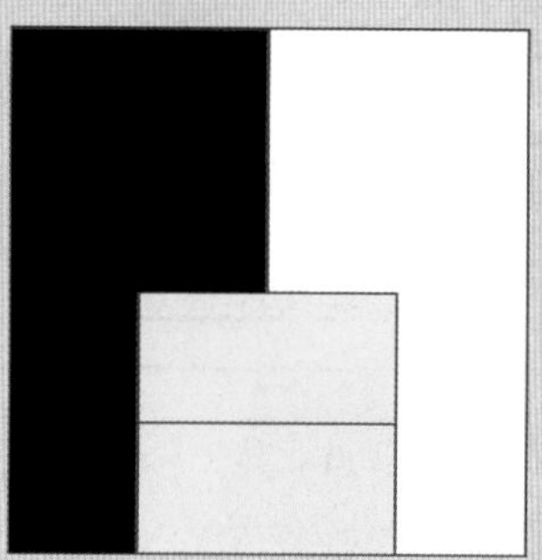

The Goddess of New York:
Part One – IX/1, 2007

The Goddess of New York:
Part Three – 1/2, 2007

Diptych: *Death Is Light Sans Serif and No "I"*
(The Orphic Font, Part Three), 2007

Gross Boy Peter (The ego-"I"), 90,
from *The Struwwelpeter Suite (The ego-"I" and The Straightener): Contemplating The Mind/Body Problem and The Bodily Illusion Of Being a Separate "self", Part One*, 2008

The Self-Illumination Of Harriet
(The Insufficiency Of A Merely Mental Enlightenment), 47,
from *The Struwwelpeter Suite (The ego-"I" and The Straightener): Contemplating The Mind/Body Problem and The Bodily Illusion Of Being a Separate "self", Part Three*, 2008

Childish Conrad and The Evil Thumb-Tailor,
or, The Boogeyman Always Bobs Both
(It Is Your Fear What Takes The Life Out Of You,
Because The Mind Always Deceives The Body), 12,
from *The Struwwelpeter Suite (The ego-"I" and The Straightener):*
Contemplating The Mind/Body Problem
and The Bodily Illusion Of Being a Separate "self",
Part Six, 2008

XVII.

Open-Handed Image-Art

It is significant that among the earliest art-forms human beings ever made are images of open hands. The artist would apparently put a hand up against a cave wall and blow contrasting materials out of the mouth (thus creating a silhouette of the hand), or (otherwise) immerse the hand in a contrasting material and press the hand on the wall (thus leaving an impression of the hand).

Such images of open hands are among the oldest art that still exists. And, indeed, the quality of open-handedness—in the sense of freedom from the "self"-contraction of egoic existence—does, in fact, have something to do with why people in prehistoric times would blow contrasting material around their hands or put hand-impressions on cave walls, and with why anybody might do so now.

The breath and the hand—that happening-conjunction says something about what right and true art is.

Right and true art is an open-handedness—not a closed fist, not a dissociated or "self"-contracted gesture.

Right and true art flows to the viewer—rather than being at war with the viewer, or aggressively trying to control and defeat the viewer.

Altogether, right and true art enables and serves the viewer—in an open-handed, ego-transcending manner.

Right and true art is infinitely generous.

XVIII.

The Tree of Human Shape: My Image-Art of Indivisible Form

A tree exemplifies the self-organizing principle of growth and change in the context of space and time. Because a tree grows (or, in fact, moves) slowly in space and time, its structure (or physical form) is the direct formal evidence of the total (unified, integrated, and indivisible) process of its living in space and time.

The human entity is a structure that, in its essentials, exists (from birth) as a pre-established form—before the process of living in space and time (outside the womb) commences. The human entity departs from the mother's womb pre-formed for life. By contrast, the tree emerges into the world as a seed—and the world (of elements, and of space, and of time) is its lifetime womb.

In the process of living in space and time, the human entity demonstrates the effects of experience and change by reactions indicated on and against its pre-formed structure, which (as such) engages, and suffers, and endures the lifetime of efforts, blows, and events. By contrast, the tree's actual structure is, itself, made in and by the life-process of experience, adaptation, and change.

This formal difference between human entities and trees is a kind of metaphor, which directly describes (or indicates, by means of form alone) the difference between the human appearance and the possibility of art.

I propose a formal approach to making and doing image-art that begins with (and consistently responds to) the appearances, conditions, and experiences of human life—and, on that basis, responsively generates forms that are a unified, integrated, and indivisible formal demonstration of the totality-all-at-once. In this image-art, the "human" is the source, and the "tree" is the idea, or the mode of pattern wherein and whereby the human totality of experience is shown by an indivisible formal summary in-response.

XIX.

How To Be The Surface Space of My Image-Art

The "surface" space of the images I make and do is not "objective" space.

The space of the images I make and do need not be "entered into"—as if the "viewer" is not always already "there", in the "surface" space itself.

In the "surface" space of the images I make and do, no means—such as familiar and conventionally recognizable elements, or other "vehicles" (such as human likenesses) expected to "represent" the "viewer" in the "surface" space of the image—are required in order to un-"lock" the "surface" space of the images, and (thus) transport (or "escort") the "viewer" (or the space-time-"located" and altogether separate and detached "point of view") to in.

The "surface" space of the images I make and do is Subjective "Space".

The "viewer" (or would-be "point of view") is—in and As Intrinsically egoless, Non-separate, and Indivisible Reality Itself—always already in, of, and As (or Perfectly Non-separate from) the "surface" space of the images I make and do.

The ego-"I", or (always space-time-"located") "point of view", cannot itself enter (or be in, of, and As) the "surface" space of the images I make and do—because the "surface" space Is the Intrinsically egoless, Non-separate, and Indivisible Subjective (and, thus, Non-"objective") "Space" of Reality Itself.

Therefore, it is in the transcending of (always space-time-"located") "point of view" (or ego-"I") itself that the "viewer"—entirely by means of tacit (or pre-mental, and purely perceptual) feeling-participation in the images I make and do—discovers and "inhabits" the "surface" space of the images I place before the bodily eyes of every one, and all.

The images I make and do are means for the "viewer" to responsively recognize and "inhabit"—and, in the moment of ego-transcending feeling-response, to sympathetically Be—the Perfectly Subjective "Space" That Is Reality Itself.

XX.

You Are The Surface Space of My Image-Art

Adi Da Samraj working on *Geome One: Alberti's Window*.

1.

In some cases, the images I make and do include familiar visual content (such as human figures, and so on), while, in other cases, the images are entirely abstract, without any obvious reference to familiar visual content. It may be felt by some "viewers" that they are "drawn in" to the images that include familiar content, whereas they are not thus "drawn in" by the entirely abstract images. This sense—of not being "drawn in" by unfamiliar (or abstract) imagery—is the result of relating to the images from the "position" of the "viewer" who presumes to be separate from the images. Indeed, people characteristically look at art from a presuming-to-be-separate "point of view"—and, in fact, people tend to look at one another, and even everything altogether, from that same "point of view".

The image-art I make and do is not in the conventional mode of art as "object" separate from the "viewer" as "subject". Rather, the image-art I make and do is about the egoless Perfect "Space" of Reality Itself, or egoless Coincidence with Reality Itself. Thus, the image-art I make and do is not purposed to provide the means for the conventional "objectification" and analytical (or merely detached) "onlooker-viewing" of art.

2.

The image-art I make and do—whether or not it includes "recognizable" content—is not "objective" space. In contrast, art as it is usually made is explicitly conceived as "objective" space—standing over against the "point of view" of the observer, as "object" to the "viewing-subject". That is the conventional notion relative to art. That is Alberti's space. Alberti described the surface of a painting as a kind of "window" through which the "viewer" would see the "outer world". Thus, by his description, not only is the surface of the artwork representational—representing something "outside" itself, or beyond and past itself—but it is "objective". In other words, Alberti was describing art based on "point of view".

I have given the title "Alberti's Window" to the suite *Geome One* as a means of pointing out that the image-art I make and do is, in fact, not Alberti's kind of space, not the traditional space of

Western art—which (first) "objectifies" the surface of the artwork, and (then) uses various devices to draw the "viewer" into the "objectified" surface. Such is the fundamental convention of art-viewing into which Westerners have been educated.

The indivisible coincidence of the "viewer" (or the "subject") and the work of art (or the visible "object") is fundamental to the communication I am making in *Alberti's Window*. In contrast to the "window" described by Alberti, the *Geome One* suite is not rendered via the conventions of perspective. Thus, the imagery of *Alberti's Window* is not based on the presumed "difference" between "subject" (or that which sees) and "object" (or that which is seen). Rather, I have made *Alberti's Window* as a communication of the absolute coincidence (or utter non-"difference") of "subject" and "object". Such coincidence (or non-"difference") of "subject" and "object" is the transcending of "point of view" altogether.

In creating *Alberti's Window*, I made photographs of the view through a window as the visual starting-point—like a sketchbook, and a key to unlock feeling-memory—and, then, I made complex abstractions in response to all of that (and more). However, in its final form, *Alberti's Window* is not merely "landscape". Indeed, it could be said that *Alberti's Window* represents the transcending of conventional notions of landscape. The imagery in *Alberti's Window* does not follow the rules of perspective, nor does it presume the usual "subject-object" orientation, as if actually looking through a window to "outside". In *Alberti's Window*, the surface itself is the domain of the event that is the image.

Thus, the imagery of *Alberti's Window* is not merely about the natural world in and of itself, nor is it merely about the natural world as it may be perceived. Rather, the imagery of *Alberti's Window* is about the perceiver, the "knower", the experiencer—and the transcending of the usual experiencer's reduction of Reality to "subject"-versus-"object", the transcending of the ego's impulse to "objectify" all perceptions.

My every work of image-art is made to convey and assist the egoless comprehension of Reality Itself. If you participate most profoundly in the images I make, you can tacitly feel and enjoy the process of that comprehension.

3.

When people speak about art, they characteristically speak from the "point of view" of presumed separateness from the art. They are viewing art as an "objective something" (over against their separate "point-of-view" position), and (thus) talking about the art from a distance.

The real aesthetic process and experience is a matter of participation—not a matter of "objectifying" and explaining art. However, in the common world of the present time, the non-participatory ego has become absolutely divorced from the apparent "object" that is the world altogether—and even from the (Intrinsically, Non-"objective") "object" that is Reality Itself.

My image-art specifically transcends the ego's impulse to "objectify". My images are not merely intended to be either a description or a criticism of the ego-position. My images are intended to subvert the entire "field" of egoic awareness (and of ego-culture, or "point-of-view" culture)—and, thus and thereby, to directly free and enable the "viewer" to transcend "point of view" (or fixed space-time-"locatedness") and (on that basis) to feel and perceive beyond the "field" of "objective" limitations.

Thus, it is helpful for people to understand that they need not approach the images I make and do in the conventional manner, which is based on standing in the ego-position. My image-art carries with it a calling for people to go beyond the ego-position and enter into egoless coincidence with Reality Itself. My image-art is a means to serve that process—through unguarded feeling-perception and full feeling-participation.

My intention in creating image-art is to use the "aesthetic experience" of "significant form" as a means of moving people, by means of their feeling-response, to go beyond "point of view" (or the uninspected paradigm of separate "subject" and separate "object").

Therefore, right participation in the image-art I make and do requires at least a tacit understanding that the "surface" space of the images I make and do is not "objective" space. Rather, the "surface" space of the images I make and do is the Perfectly Subjective "Space" of Reality Itself. For this reason, it is not necessary that I introduce familiar visual content as a means of drawing the "viewer" into the "surface" space.

The "viewer"—prior to "point of view", or ego-"I"—is already in, of, and As the "surface" space of the image-art I make and do. The "surface" space of the image-art I make and do is not "objective". The "surface" space of the image-art I make and do is Perfectly Subjective—and must be discovered to Be So. Thus, I use the image-active means of the "aesthetic experience" (and the means intrinsic to "significant form" itself) to draw "viewers" beyond the separative position of "point of view" (or ego-"I"), into the Inherently and Perfectly Subjective "Space" of Reality Itself—through artistically governed perceptual presentations.

There is a mode of right participation in the image-art I make and do which is not merely a play upon the "subject-object" condition of conventional egoic perception. I do not expect people to undertake a lengthy course of study or to develop a sophisticated philosophical understanding in order to view the images I make and do. Right participation in the image-art I make and do is, primarily, a tacit (or wordless) feeling matter.

4.

Fundamentally, the images I make and do are simply to be felt. It is the perceptually-based feeling-response—and not merely an intellectual understanding—that is required. When you are viewing the images, take the time to simply, tacitly feel them—without trying to think of something to say about them. You do not have to "figure them out". Simply participate in the images, by means of unguarded feeling-perception.

You do not have to apply any intellectual means in order simply to look at the image-art I make and do. In fact, the intellectual approach is, basically, a method for keeping the art "objectified", and keeping yourself separate from it.

Altogether, the "viewer" is called to participate in the image-art I make and do by means of feeling-responsiveness, rather than by means of talk. Well-considered discussion of art certainly has its legitimate purpose—but if you make talk the primary means by which you experience art, then you are no longer able to experience the art itself.

In this scientific materialist epoch, everything is so "objectified" that, as a general rule, people no longer presume there is any necessity to truly participate in art (or anything else). The dominance of scientific materialist dogma, and over-reliance on intellect (and strategies of control) altogether, have led to people becoming completely dissociated from the Intrinsically egoless, Non-separate, and Indivisible Self-Nature, Self-Condition, and Self-State That Is Reality Itself. So people imagine that Reality Itself does not even exist anymore, that Reality Itself is somehow "locked away" in outdated religions, that Reality Itself was, in fact, a myth.

Reality Itself is not a myth. I send the image-art I make and do into the world to serve everyone to Awaken from this hellish dissociativeness that is the ego-"I" (or space-time-bound "point of view"). My images are a means for people simply to respond in a feeling manner, to Awaken into the Perfectly Subjective "Space" that is the "surface" space of the images I make and do.

5.

By participating, in an unguarded manner, in the image-art I make and do, you allow yourself to be positively and deeply affected (and, at least for the moment, changed) by the art. Typically, people do not allow this to occur—and, in fact, the understanding that the purpose of right and true art is to positively and deeply affect and change the "viewer" has largely been lost (especially in the context of gross "public reality" culture). Rather than talking about the art, interpreting it, explaining it, simply look at it, and—by means of perceptually-governed feeling—openly participate in it. That simple looking and participating is how you gain real access to the "aesthetic experience" of "significant form". Indeed, the "aesthetic experience"—which is a kind of ecstasy (or of standing prior to separateness, prior to the ego-"I", prior to the space-time-"locatedness" of "point of view", prior to "objects", and prior to the limits of "objectified" world)—is the fundamental and necessary purpose of right and true art.

The constant effort to interpret and explain—or the notion that you must first comprehend elaborate interpretations and explanations, before you can participate in the art—actually becomes a means of detaching yourself from the participatory perceptual feeling-experience of the art itself.

My image-art is sacred—in the most profound sense of that word, the root-meaning of which is "set apart". My image-art is not sacred in the "religious" sense—not at all. Rather, it is sacred because it is offered as a means of serving the Awakening to That Which Is Great, or Reality Itself. My image-art has nothing to do with religion. My image-art is about the inherent sacredness, the intrinsic holiness, or set-apartness, of Reality Itself—"set apart" not meaning "separate", but meaning "rightly protected", such that access to it is granted only under right and appropriate conditions.

Right participation in the images I make and do requires the transcending of egoity. How do you do that? Feeling-response is the means. It is not that feeling-response allows you to "enter into" the domain of the image-art I make and do. Rather, feeling-response awakens you in, of, and as the very context—or "surface" space—of the image-art I make and do. Therefore, right (feeling-perceptual) participation is the means by which the "viewer" can be already in, of, and as the "surface" space of the image-art I make and do—rather than having to be "drawn in" by some particular characteristics of the artwork (such as visual familiarity).

6.

The importance of unguarded and feeling-responsive perceptual participation is the reason why I fabricate images in monumental scale. If an image is "smalled down", the "viewer" can, in some sense, consume it, or contain it, or control it. Thus, the largeness of the images is entirely intentional. The monumentality enables the art to break down the barriers that ego generates to keep itself separate. If the art is big enough—in every sense, not only with reference to physical size—then the "viewer" cannot merely "objectify" it, and the feeling-responses will inevitably come to the fore.

There is a great difference between, on the one hand, picking up a work of art that is printed in a book at the rather small size of, say, eight by ten inches and, on the other hand, being suddenly confronted by a twenty-foot gorilla. I am not saying that the images I make and do are like fierce and threatening gorillas—but a twenty-foot gorilla immediately cancels anything you might want to say, and your feeling-responsiveness is such that you have to "deal with" the situation. So it is with the monumental images I make and do—the "viewer's" positively unguarded feeling-responsiveness will inevitably come to the fore, replacing the "explanation-mind" that would otherwise tend to "objectify" the art and keep it at a distance. Nevertheless, the right, and true, and truly unguarded perceptual feeling-response to the image-art I make and do is not a "fight or flight" response (as when faced by a twenty-foot gorilla), but, rather, it is the ecstatic response of non-separate and non-dissociative coincidence with the Perfectly Subjective "surface" space of the image itself.

7.

My image-art, in every respect, calls for participation. Such participation is not merely a matter of going beyond the surface of representational art, as in Alberti's space. My image-art is not pointing to something beyond itself. My image-art is created as a pointer to itself—As a manifestation (and As an Intrinsically Perfect Moment) of Reality Itself.

Therefore, the perceptible "surface" space of the image-art I make and do is the Perfectly Subjective "Space" of Reality Itself—Which Exists in only one place, Reality Itself. Whether or not I use familiar visual content, such as human figures, and so forth, it is still the same "Space"—the "Space" of Reality Itself. My image-art is not pointing to something else—even though, paradoxically, it may (because of sometimes somehow familiar references) seem to be doing so.

Try to enter into the "surface" space of any of the images I have made. Where would you possibly go? You cannot "get into" that space, because it is not the space of "point of view". In order to be in the "surface" space of the image-art I make and do, you must transcend "point of view"—and perceptually-based feeling-response is how that is done.

Feeling-response is pre-verbal. Feeling-response is not merely in the world of the unconscious, as depicted in surrealist art. Rather, fundamental feeling-response is in the very context of perception itself. Perception itself is the pre-verbal domain of Reality Itself, the Indivisible and Non-separate domain of egolessness. Therefore, the domain of right feeling-participation in the image-art I make and do is not the domain of depth-ego (or "internal subjectivity"), but the realm of perceptual seeing. Unguarded perceptual seeing—enacted via unobstructed (and inherently "self"-forgetting) feeling—is the always immediate means of being "always already entered" into the "surface" space of the image-art I make and do. And that "doorway" of unguarded perceptual feeling-participation is the always immediate "doorway" to Reality Itself—Which Is Always Already As Is.

8.

Reality Itself is always the "Surface" of existence.

Reality Itself is always immediate to the perceptual view, as long as "point of view" is transcended.

Reality Itself Is Where and As you Really Are.

The ego-"I" is always one foot (or more) away from the "Surface" that Is Reality Itself.

The ego-"I" is always living in the illusory presumption that "objects" are "not-self".

My image-art is not made and done to reflect and entertain the ego-"self".

My image-art is made and done to perceptually embody—and, thus, by means of the "aesthetic experience" of "significant form", to communicate—the Intrinsically egoless, Non-separate, and Indivisible Self-Nature, Self-Condition, Self-State, and Perfectly Subjective "Space" That Is Reality Itself.

XXI.

The Open-Eyed Room

1. The "inner self" (and the psycho-physical totality of ego-"I") is (always, and inherently) a form of representation—a psycho-physical construction of perceptions, perceptual-conceptual responses and reactions, and both perceptual and conceptual reveries played upon the base of all of that.

2. The "inner self" (and the psycho-physical totality of ego-"I") is a brain-structured (and, altogether, a neurologically-structured) mere chaos of permutations of centerless random reflections—but the brain-mind always works to represent that randomly changing chaos as a centered integrity, via the constant enforcement (or perpetual internal iteration) of the illusory psycho-physical invention (or representational device) of a "point-of-view"-identity.

3. Always Perfectly Prior to the ego-"self" Is the Intrinsic (formless, centerless, egoless, Non-separate, and Indivisible) Self-Condition That Is Reality Itself—or the Non-representational (and Never-"objectified") Source-Condition That Is the Consciousness-Energy Medium and Transcendental egoless Self-Identity of the otherwise egoically-represented body-mind-complex and the (egoically-presumed) "objective" world.

4. The ego-"I" is a neurologically-projected interior representation, spontaneously self-organized moment to moment—and never as a permanently configured "icon" of "self", but always by an active re-morphing of its own figure, by means of perceptual and conceptual changes in the brain-projected (or, altogether, neurologically-projected) illusory ego-center, or discrete and separate "point of view".

5. The ego-"I" is always an illusory invention, always a temporarily constructed representation (or psycho-physical fabrication), which, as an implication of its own perpetual changefulness, always suggests (as the very core of the egoic "self"-illusion) that an independent, separate center permanently "self"-exists—as the would-be "I" (or even the metaphysic "soul", or "ghost", or "inner spirit") that is the neurologically-projected "self"-center (or discrete and separate "point of view").

6. The perpetually changing ego-"I"-form (both bodily and mentally represented) and its implied permanent interior of "point of view" are both illusions (or mere representations)—mere and insubstantial conventions, or neurologically-invented and psycho-physically fabricated perceptual-conceptual pseudo-"objects", seeming to compose a persona of separate identity, as a "mummer" (or a temporarily-invented "self") in an otherwise chaotic, and intrinsically egoless (or centerless, non-discrete, and non-separate), "play" of interior neuro-perceptual sensations and brain-encoded words.

7. The ego-"I" (or total psycho-physical "point-of-view"-illusion, or invention, or fabrication, or mere representation) is an inherently related "entity" (or pseudo-identity), existing always and only in the context of a "mummery theatre" of associations, both within the interior of the body-mind-"self" and in the apparent exterior within which the body-mind-"self" is projected (or "self"-presumed and "self"-understood to be an active persona).

8. The totality of the ego-"I"-persona (of neurologically-based "self"-representation) is always accompanied, surrounded, supported, and defined by its "company"—a complex collection (or "self"-accumulated "mummery theatre") of interiorly-projected representations, in the form of "others" (and every kind of "object"), and in the comprehensive form of an ideated (and always changing) world.

9. All the "self"-represented relations of the "self"-represented ego-"I" are, variously, the ego-supporting, and ego-threatening, and always (in effect) ego-defining (or "point-of-view"-characterizing) dramatis personae of the egoically-"objectified" interior and exterior of the "world-mummery" of ego's always presumed-to-be-separate "point of view".

10. My art of image (and, also, the literary art I make and do) addresses, altogether inspects, comprehends, and (by artistic means) demonstrates the always Prior Reality-transcending of the egoic "self"-representation, all egoically-defined "others" and "objects", and the totality of "world-mummery" that is the always representational "theatre" of ego-based experience.

11. Fundamentally, the image-art I make and do is, itself, a perceptual demonstration of the Intrinsically egoless, Non-representational, Non-separate, and Indivisible Open-Eyed "Room" of Conscious Light That Is the Always Prior and Perfect Self-Condition of Reality Itself, and (Thus and Therefore) of all conditionally arising appearances, and of all subsequent perceptual and conceptual representations of conditionally arising appearances.

12. The Open-Eyed "Room" of Conscious Light Is the One and Self-Existing Space of Truth's No-Mummery—and all the image-art I make and do is sent to Self-Illuminate upon Its Walls of Happen, and of Happen's tearless Equanimity.

XXII.

The Beautiful Room of Perfect Space

The art I make and do has a profound purpose. Therefore, the art I make and do can only be fully rightly viewed within a context that supports that purpose.

I have been working artistically since childhood—but I quickly became aware that the necessary cultural basis for the making and viewing of art, in its true profundity, was uniquely lacking in the "post-modern" world. Therefore, I worked for many decades to establish the basis for a new world-culture, founded in the fullest right understanding of life and of Reality (Itself, and altogether). Only since I fundamentally completed that foundation-work have I been free to concentrate intensively in the (now, fully rightly culturally-founded) making and doing of art.

By its very nature, the art I make and do confronts people—because the art I make and do is intended to move people beyond their tendency to "objectify" whatever is in front of them and to detach themselves from it (even in order to "control" the art, and, thus, to desensitize themselves to its possible profound impact upon them). Therefore, the art I make and do must be presented in such a manner that people are moved and free to participate in it—and, thus, to allow the art to be a life-transforming participatory experience.

The art I make and do should always be presented in such a manner that the mode of presentation directly (and really effectively) overwhelms the convention-bound tendency to reduce the art to the status of a mere "object"—small, contained, controllable, and (thus) "objectified" to such a degree that the viewer is "protected" (or, in effect, immunized) against the "aesthetic experience" itself (and "significant form" itself). The art I make and do should always be presented in such a manner that the viewer is never "protected" (or detached and, thereby, immunized) from the possible transformative—physical, emotional, psychological, intellectual, moral, and otherwise most profound and life-transforming—effect of the inherently and necessarily participatory event (or the real and true "aesthetic experience", rather than the mere "thing") of the art I make and do. However, to truly move people beyond the habitual (and, in general, now culturally institutionalized) "objectification" of art—and the awful convention of mental (and even total psycho-physical) detachment from it, and (altogether) the always all-limiting tendency toward ego-based association with it—requires modes of art-presentation that are uniquely conceived, carefully enacted, and truly effective.

The twentieth century was a period of the global collapse of the old (and even ancient) foundations and structures of civilization and culture. Thus, from the beginning of the twentieth century until World War II, the old order of civilization and culture was disintegrating and approaching its death. The period encompassed by World War II accomplished the death of the old order of civilization and culture. For the two decades that included and followed World War II, the death of the old order of civilization and culture was the subject of reaction and regret (including much denial, anger, bargaining, depression, and resignation). Then, from the 1960s to the turn of the twenty-first century, there was a period of virtual non-civilization and non-culture. And only now is the moment for the emerging of the truly new.

Based on this synopsis of the twentieth century, the century can be divided into three periods of cultural and artistic evidence: the period of "modernism" (1900–1940), the period of transition to "post-modernism" (1940–1960), and the fully "post-modernist" period (or "dark epoch") of no-culture and non-art (1960–2001).

The entire culture of the world-tradition of art changed in the near-middle of the twentieth century. World War II (which completed and finalized the effects of World War I) had everything to do with this change—which is characterized by the collapse of the totality of the world-culture of civilization, the collapse of the traditional understanding of Reality and Truth, and, as a result, the collapse of the capability for (and even the valuing of) the "aesthetic experience" of "significant form". Some good art continued to be made in the second half of the twentieth century, by certain unique individuals—but, in general, following World War II, there was a general breakdown in the culture of art, reflecting the breakdown in the civilization-culture of the world altogether.

I have no impulse to make and do art on the basis of the "post-modern" (or even "post-civilization") cultural breakdown. That is why I worked so intensively to re-establish a basis for a

Reality-culture, a Truth-culture—before I could intensively make and do art within the context of an actual and living culture of Reality and Truth.

The "modernist" artists who functioned in the earlier part of the twentieth century, before World War II, were, regardless of their otherwise revolutionary ideas and methods, yet participating in (or at least playing upon) a culture and a tradition of fundamental great virtue, that was (historically) already long-established in the context of the "aesthetic experience" (and, altogether, in the context of traditional greater matters of aspiration). However, even before the devastating effects of World War II, the cultural breakdown of world-civilization was initiated by the profound effects of World War I. Altogether, the twentieth century was a progressive anti-cultural and de-civilizing process, that has (in those terms) worked the world-devastation of every aspect of the entire great tradition of humankind. There were great achievements in the twentieth century, but there was also, more essentially, the universal destruction (or negative transformation) of the world-civilization of human life and culture. There was more great virtue at the beginning of the twentieth century than at the end—and, yet, what was occurring at the beginning of the twentieth century was also part of (and coincident with) the progressively emerging breakdown of world-culture and of the great human process.

There are many uniquely important (and, indeed, truly and positively revolutionary) elements in the culture and art of "modernism" which were interrupted after the end of World War II (and especially post-1960). However, I regard the many uniquely important elements in the culture and art of "modernism" to be the roots of a profoundly transformative and artistically liberating renewal of the entire world-tradition of making and doing art. It is, therefore, necessary that the "liberating instant" of "modernism" be continued, and always further developed, and even (hopefully) exceeded—but, certainly, not merely renounced and forever lost in the "post-modern" and the, now, "post-civilization", and "post-culture", era (or "dark epoch", or "late-time") of conventional (gross) "realism", anti-art, post-art, non-art, and every other kind and degree of counter-aestheticism, anti-aestheticism, and social, cultural, and political nihilism.

The term "post-modernism" was, originally (and appropriately), proposed in reference to particular changes in later-twentieth-century architecture—and not in reference to the fine arts (of painting, sculpture, and so on). The extending of the term "post-modernism" to the fine arts is a false (and, in general, negatively influential) effort that has resulted in the general reduction of the fine arts (including all that must qualify as true "high art") to a "low art" happening, in which the fine arts have been made indistinguishable from popular (and, in general, socio-political) cultural artifacts and nihilistic "post-civilization" activities.

So-called "post-modernism" (following Duchamp, et al.) is an anti-artistic (and profoundly anti-aesthetic) aberration that directly opposes the great human tradition of rooted-in-perception true and "high" art. In the "post-modernist" domain, art and life have been mixed together to such a degree that all "art" is reduced to the status of an intrinsically "low" art, or a mere "reality-artifact" of popular (and reductively quotidian) culture, society, and politics.

The "post-modernist" agenda is grounded in groundless irony, divorced—by egoic and (altogether) mental, psychological, and darkly "intellectual" preoccupations—from the perceptual equanimity that is the necessary characteristic of true "aesthetic experience".

Right, true, and (at least potentially) "high" art is, by contrast to "post-modernist" artifacts (and all of "low art", pseudo-art, and anti-art), grounded in profoundest perceptual equanimity, and in a comprehensive depth of apprehension of its "subject", and (no matter what the "subject" or the depth of feeling may coincidently convey) it is always pervaded and supported by the intrinsic joy and sublimity that demonstrates the true "aesthetic experience" of "significant form"—even such that all irony is vanished from its heart.

Therefore, it is now necessary for the entire happening of "post-modernism" in the fine arts to be culturally passed beyond, and replaced by the right and true culture and activity of authentic fine art—including authentic "high art", upon which the authentic process of right and true human civilization necessarily (and only in part, but, nonetheless, very significantly, and indispensably) depends.

The art I make and do re-establishes the (necessary) right and true connection to the great (and total) world-tradition of art—including, necessarily, pre-World-War-II "modernism". I am making art that is intended to be fine art of greatest (and truly "high art") significance and transformative power—art that invites profound participation, rather than the mode of casual and dissociated viewing that allows and supports (and even requires, and, ultimately, even institutionalizes) mere "objectification" and dissociative (or strategically non-participatory) detachment. I want to transform people's participation in art—and also their participation in Reality (Itself, and altogether)—and help bring them to a new way of life, out of the "dark" period in which humankind is presently immersed.

For some decades now, there has been a trend of opinion in some parts of the art world that "beauty" is some kind of taboo. Why should real and true beauty be taboo? The "aesthetic experience" (including the necessary great and sublime perceptual experience of real and true beauty) is not merely a "nice idea". Rather, the "aesthetic experience" of "significant form", and (thus and thereby) of real and true beauty—or the aesthetic and artistic Self-Manifestation of The Beautiful (Itself)—is a human necessity, even fundamental to the structure of the human body-mind-complex. The "aesthetic experience" of "significant form" (and, thus and thereby, of real and true beauty) is neurologically based—pre-"wired" into the human nervous system and brain. Any counter-aesthetic (or anti-aesthetic) effort (or any effort that opposes, or runs counter to, the "beauty-wired" aspect of the human structure) is, in effect, a form of abuse of the human being—and of the necessary right acculturation of humankind as a whole.

The true (and traditional) purpose of art is to draw the human being into the sphere of "significant form" via the "aesthetic experience"—in which the entire brain and nervous system, and (indeed) the entire body-mind and active life, is profoundly "tuned" to Reality (Itself, and altogether), and Truth (Itself, and altogether), and Beauty (or The Beautiful, Itself, and altogether). The (necessarily, participatory) psycho-physical condition of being "tuned" to Reality (Itself, and altogether) and Truth (Itself, and altogether) Is the "aesthetic experience" of Real and True Beauty (or The Beautiful, Itself, and altogether) in, as, and via "significant form". There is a human necessity for a kind of resonation of vibratory participation in Reality (Itself, and altogether), and Truth (Itself, and altogether), and Beauty (or The Beautiful, Itself, and altogether)—beyond conventional "yes" and "no", beyond conventional "beauty" and conventional "ugliness", beyond conventional "realism", and beyond egoity altogether. Such human profundity is a great and necessary purpose, which true art (and, altogether, true culture and right civilization) should and must serve.

The purpose of the art I make and do is to serve the acculturation (and, as may be required, the transformative restoration) of human beings to participation in true profundity. Therefore, the art I make and do should be viewed in a profound right setting. Ideally, the right setting is a kind of (even, perhaps, literally) "spherical" space—a comprehensive space that transcends (or requires the transcending of) the conventions of "subject" and "object"—with the aesthetic force and capability to move the perceiver beyond "point of view" (or the egoic "self"-position, presumed to be irreducibly separate from whatever "other", or "object", is presumed to be "outside" itself). Such a "spherical" space functions as an all-surrounding and (yet) all-liberating circumstance, in which the presumption of separate "self" (or ego-"I"), and the egoic illusion of separate "object", and even all the consequences of "point of view" are (simultaneously) undermined—by the "spherically-evident" profundity of Reality (Itself, and altogether). Thus, the viewing of the art I make and do should be an immersive experience, which moves the viewer beyond the presumption of limits, beyond the capability to "control" the art, the artistic environment, and the "aesthetic experience" altogether. The necessary space required for fullest right participation in the art I make and do is (and must be) beyond the possibility of that ("subjective") "stepping-back"-from-the-art that (first) "objectifies" the art and (then) escapes from the "sphere" of the "aesthetic experience" itself and of "significant form" itself.

The art I make and do is intended to challenge the viewer, in a manner that allows for real (and even total) life-transformation.

Therefore, the art I make and do must be presented in a manner that supports, rather than minimizes, its inherent demand on the viewer.

Previous to the twentieth century, there were essentially two forms of "high art"—the religious and the secular. In religious art, the sacred is given "official" limits by the prevailing religious tradition—whereas in secular art, the artifices and personalities of political and social power are given iconic status by means of the application of otherwise religious artifices to secular "subjects".

In the "modernist" tradition of the early twentieth century, a new, (and, potentially, sacred) art emerged as a possibility—an art of profundity, free of both "official" religion and merely secular impulses. However, it was, first, necessary for the old (religious and secular) culture to pass away. Thus, at the start of the twenty-first century, the old culture was, in fundamental terms, dead and gone—and only a global non-culture remained. Therefore, now is the moment for the emergence of a new order of both civilization and culture—and, thus, for the emergence of a new, and truly sacred (non-religious, non-secular, and Really non-egoic), art.

A traditional (or old-culture) temple or church is an example of a space—or even an institutional art-form—intended as a place for people to go when they feel a need to deal profoundly with something in themselves that is difficult (even to the degree of not being otherwise amenable to human efforts toward resolution). A traditional temple or church is a kind of architecture of psychological enclosure, even a kind of "holy womb", if you like—a kind of "iconic space" (or old-culture-based "sacred sphere"), beyond the otherwise "non-sacred", or secular, or profane space of the body (in and of itself). A traditional temple or church is culturally and artistically purposed to open up (by means of the old-culture forms of "aesthetic experience") into something beyond—a life-transforming space that is profoundly protective, and (yet) demanding. A traditional temple or church is a place where people are supposed to go in order not to talk a lot, and not to do things arbitrarily. In a traditional temple or a church, people are, instead, expected to conform to what is <u>required</u> of "self" by what is beyond "self"—and which confronts the "self" with its influence (or the culturally-enacted intrusion of what is beyond "self") by means of architecture, and by means of artistically-rendered words and images, and by means of the old-culture forms of "sacred activities" that are (even theatrically) enacted in the old-culture-based "sacred space". Rightly, a traditional temple or a church is supposed to be entered with the intent to participate in something beyond the separate "self"—something inherently and truly profound.

Generally speaking, the places where the art I make and do is to be exhibited would not be traditional (or old-culture) temples or churches. The art I make and do is not to be associated with any old-culture form of either conventional religion or gross secularism—but the art I make and do is, inherently (and by means of its every intended purpose), associated with Reality (Itself, and altogether). Therefore, any environment in which the art I make and do is exhibited should be a truly (and not merely "officially") "sacred enclosure" (or a unique comprehensive environment, or "sphere") that supports any and every viewer's true and wholly non-"protected" (and, altogether, new-culture) participation in Reality (Itself, and altogether).

The purpose of the art I make and do is to "assist" the viewer in the profound (and rightly "subjective") process of participating in Reality (Itself, and altogether)—beyond all effort to "objectify", beyond separate "self", beyond mind, beyond mere "talk", and (altogether) beyond "point of view". Therefore, the entire exhibition-environment should be conducive to that inherently transformational process.

The art I make and do is, by its very nature, transformational art. There are many different legitimate purposes for which art can be made and done—but the art I make and do has an inherent association with the intrinsically transformative profundity of Reality (Itself, and altogether), and (therefore) with the profundity of (necessarily, life-transforming) participation in Reality (Itself, and altogether).

The art I make and do is (itself) the transformational environment of free participation in Reality Itself and in Reality altogether—an open space, a field of light, a space beyond limitations, purposed to draw the viewer beyond the illusions of "difference" that otherwise appear to be separate "self", and separate "object", and separate "other", and separate "world".

The art I make and do Is the Perfect Space.

The art I make and do Is the Beautiful "Room".

XXIII.

The Varietal Characteristic of "Reality" In Modernism, Post-Modernism, and Transcendental Realism

"Modernists"—such as Malevich, Kandinsky, Mondrian, and Rothko—proposed a kind of pictographically symbolized "platonic" (or "spiritual", meaning essentially non-material) "reality" as an alternative to the otherwise perceived gross "reality" of bodily and material awareness.

Other "modernists"—beginning with the "cubists" (including Braque, Picasso, Gris, and others), and, then, on to the "surrealists" (such as Dalí, Miró, de Chirico, Magritte, and even Bacon) and the "abstract expressionists" (such as Pollock and de Kooning)—engaged in pictorial efforts to analyze, de-construct, and re-construct gross (and grossly psychologized) perceptual "reality", and (thus and thereby) demonstrated a fundamental "spiritual" (or "subjectively" conflicted) anxiety about the human condition.

In contrast to the "modernists", the post-"modernists"—even beginning with Duchamp, and on to the "pop" artists (such as Warhol and Lichtenstein) and such anti-"modernist" artists as Stella, Newman, Rauschenberg, and Johns—engaged in gross pictorial "realism" (or "gross reductionism" and "gross objectivism") to the point of exhausting its "charm" absolutely.

The Transcendental Realist image-art I make and do is neither a "platonic" (or "alternative-reality") exercise nor an exercise in "gross realism" (whether in the manner of "analytical deconstruction" or in the manner of "gross reductionism").

Rather, the Transcendental Realist image-art I make and do is a process based on direct apprehension (or root-apperception) of the Intrinsically egoless and Irreducibly Indivisible Self-Nature, Self-Condition, and Self-State of Reality Itself—and, thus, the image-art I make and do is a process, in aesthetic and perceptible artistic terms, of intrinsically egoless (or "point-of-view"-less, or anegoic, and aperspectival, and aniconic) coincidence with the intrinsic Reality-characteristic of all perceptual experience and, indeed, of all possible human experience.

XXIV.

The Eternal War Between Orpheus and Narcissus: The Culture of ego-Transcendence Versus The Anti-Culture of ego-Reflection

1.

In the so-called "modern era" of the twentieth and twenty-first centuries, people seem to imagine that human experience is now remarkably different, in some absolute sense, in comparison to the experience of people in previous centuries. In the "modern era", it seems to be presumed that previously unknown difficulties are now happening all of a sudden.

For this reason, it is also (and absurdly) presumed that art and culture are now (and from now on) required to be some kind of anti-art or anti-culture—or a to-the-public, by-the-public, and for-the-public reflection of the "new epoch" of "never-before-seen" negativity, emptiness, gross "realism", public-"realism" art, and a totality of art and culture thoroughly debased and desecrated by the grossly politicized mind of vulgarity's streetest dark and fireless deep of death's own inspiration.

It is now ("post-all") presumed that the experience of people in the past "allowed" them to create art that was inspiring and beautiful—whereas the experience of "modern" human beings no longer "allows" that.

It is now ("after" all) presumed that, because the "modern reality" is uniquely "different" from all past "realities", artists are not supposed to "do" beauty anymore.

It is even presumed (in the now of "nothing more") that the "aesthetic experience"—or ego-transcending and ecstatic participation in "significant form"—is no longer required, and even, somehow, no longer to be "allowed".

All of this absurdly negative presuming about history and art is simply a misreading of both history and art. The past has been just as full of dreadfulness—politically, socially, and in every sense—as "modern" times. Indeed, in some respects, the conditions in past centuries were even worse for people in general. In the "modern era", there has been far more enjoyment of the "goods of life"—for people in general—than there ever was previous to the twentieth century. In earlier times, people lived (as everyone now lives) with horrific plagues (in which vast portions of the population died, or may yet die) and (as also now) people everywhere lived in the midst of virtually constant dreadful wars. In earlier times, life was, in general, extremely difficult for most people (whereas, in the "modern era", many more have lived comparatively well). In the midst of such difficult circumstances, people in past times always made intensive use of both daily and rare beauty, and always, as total and all-inclusive cultures, made fullest use of the "aesthetic experience", and always everywhere promoted the daily use of modes of understanding that reach beyond the limits of mortality, of gross physicality, and of gross "realism". In virtually all times before "modern" times, the human need for beauty and all-transcending "self"-understanding—and the indispensability, intrinsic value, and fundamental reality of beauty and profoundest "self"-understanding—was, in general, culturally and socially acknowledged (and, at least within the sphere of those who were most intensively so-inclined, both fully appreciated and fully exercised).

Human existence is, in every fundamental sense, no different in "modern" times than at any and all other times—except that, in this "modern era", human beings have collectively arrived at some kind of agreement (or they have, certainly, been everywhere propagandized into accepting) that the great possibilities of human existence (including right and true art, and, altogether, the culture of ultimate transcendence) are no longer either relevant or acceptable. Indeed, the current propaganda is that those great possibilities should be abandoned, because "some uniquely dreadful situation exists now which human beings have never experienced before". All of that propaganda is—like the naked Emperor's traitorous tailor—utterly false. Indeed, all such propositions are merely the death-messages of ignorant anti-culture and the benighted philosophies of gross "realism".

To "set up camp" in the realm of negativity, grossest "self"-bondage, anti-culture, anti-art, the absolutized defeat of beauty, and the universal denial of the necessity for the "aesthetic experience" of "significant form", all in and by means of an intrinsically benighted and dreadful embrace of the realm and culture of gross "realism", is to fall into a downward spiral that only has nothingness, death, and darkness at its end.

For the sake of everyone and all, there must now be the retrieval of really and truly inspired culture.

The right and true (and, now and forever hereafter, necessarily global) human culture is, by definition, a universal and positively inspired human domain wherein the possibilities of transcendence and ultimacy are cultivated and developed by all.

The artistic manifestations of such a re-newed culture of inspiration will not necessarily look the same as art made in the past. In the West, the institutionally obligatory "Christian" art of past centuries is no longer a necessary mode of representation. Indeed, specifically "Christianized" art is—within the comprehensive context of world-inclusive art—merely a conventional (and sometimes "official") characteristic of "Western" tribalism, provincialism, and all-limiting culture-bondage. Likewise, in the East, all "official" (or otherwise conventionally expected) artistic traditions are based on "local" (and, altogether, "Easternized") mythologies, symbols, archetypes, histories, religions, and social biases that do not (in and of themselves) encompass the indivisible totality of truly globally-extended (and should-be-cooperative) humankind.

The fundamental (and, heretofore, perennial) great disposition that must now be universally retrieved is the disposition to exceed the limitations of mortality, egoity, and gross existence altogether. That disposition is the right and true and necessary domain of right and true art, and (altogether) of right and true culture. The world-culture of humankind as a whole needs to become re-oriented now—away from its "meditation" on the downward spiral into darkness and the myths of "end-time", and profoundly toward the disposition that would transcend all limitations.

The image-art I make and do is intended to serve the "aesthetic experience" of greatest profundity and of the intrinsic transcending of all limitations. My image-art is not religious art. My image-art is not made and done in any conventionally traditional manner. My image-art is made and done in the intrinsically free disposition that otherwise characterizes the fundamental manner of means that can be seen throughout the "modern" period and even the "post-modern" (or "aberrationist", or "absurdist") period. However, in the image-art I make and do, all kinds of free means that I have originated and developed are being put to use in the context of a unique disposition relative to doing art, and a unique understanding of the purpose of art. That purpose could be described as the "radical" (or always "at-the-root") uplifting of the human disposition—out of the grossest course of conventional "realism", and out of egoic (or space-time-"located", and divisibility-driven, and "point-of-view"-bound) "self"-delusion, and out of the absurdities of anti-beauty, and out of the "dark"-minded determination to crush the "aesthetic experience" and even every lighted sign and vestige of "significant form". In that sense, the image-art I make and do manifests the same fundamental disposition that human art has manifested for thousands of years. That anciently demonstrated disposition would transcend death, and egoity, and mortality, and gross "realism"—and all of the political and social and cultural darkness that inevitably follows upon the "philosophy" of gross "realism".

Both the image-art and the literary art I make and do are free manifestations of what I intend as right and true art—or art in the ego-transcending (or Orphic) and, altogether, Transcendental Realist mode of action, rather than in the merely ego-reflecting and gross-"realism"-bound (or Narcissistic) mode of action.

Orpheus and Narcissus are, characteristically and inherently, opposites—in forever opposition to one another. One of the forever two must die in the eternal struggle—or else neither one can win.

Narcissus (or the ego-"I") <u>must</u> die. Orpheus (or the will to ego-transcending Perfection) <u>must</u> win. Or else, the human being—or even the total culture of humankind—will die in contemplation of the mirror that is its own and mortal mind.

This "modern" time is not, in any absolute sense, different from previous times. It is simply that people in this time are tending not to make use of what is required to transcend the binding and negating force of mortal human experience. Indeed, in this "modern" time, human beings are collectively relinquishing the very means that, in all previous epochs of human history, have been used to master and go beyond the limiting power of mortal human experience.

If humankind ceases to make use of the disposition to transcend limitations—if people are somehow "talked out" of that disposition, or if that disposition is somehow culturally, socially, and politically not permitted—then the "dark" time that humankind is now suffering (and that, in every fundamental sense, shares all of the same human experiences of difficulty, stress, challenge, and limitation that humankind has suffered throughout human history) can, indeed, become an "end-time". To "cancel" the impulse to transcend limitations is a volunteering to death, to negativity, to "dark"-mindedness, to anti-culture, to nihilism—and, ultimately, to the unconscionable (and even willful) annihilation of humankind and the inexcusable destruction of all of the natural domain of Earth.

When human beings cease to make use of the means for transcending limitations, they, consequently and inevitably, bind themselves to what would, otherwise, be transcended and gone beyond. And that bondage inevitably becomes death, negation, darkness, and emptiness.

Human culture is now, collectively and globally, in the untenable position of willfully choosing to not make use of the means for transcending limitations—and of collectively choosing to globally suffer the inevitable consequences. Thus, human culture is now volunteering to be utterly brought down by chaotic and gross influences. This devastating cultural trend is evident not only in the global political and social happenings that are everywhere now so dreadful from day to day. This devastating trend is also evident in the life of each and every human individual—whatever the zones of daily existence in which any given individual participates.

To be collectively (politically, socially, and culturally) without the will and the means for transcending limitations—and, thus, altogether, to be collectively without the will and the means to go (even Ultimately and Perfectly) beyond—is the characteristic (and the "globalized" suffering) of people everywhere in the present moment of human history.

Through the image-art (and the literary art) I make and do—and also through all of the work I do altogether—I am here to undo the "dark" disposition, and to restore humankind to the disposition of transcending limitations and of Realizing the Ultimate Truth That Is (Transcendentally and Spiritually) the Intrinsically egoless, Non-separate, and Indivisible Self-Nature, Self-Condition, and Self-State of Reality Itself.

What I am working to do with the making and doing of image-art is to bring the right and true means of transcending all limitations—and of Realizing Ultimate Truth As Reality Itself—into the context of visual perception, and to actually demonstrate that all-limitation-transcending means (and That Ultimate Reality-Realization) as and by means of all the images I make and do.

2.

The Emperor's new tailor is always here a fraud.

Long live the forever naked Emperor of all of Right and True—and mock with laugh again the fraud of fashion's tailored new, that makes a show to hide or dark the Solar "Bright" of Real.

Death to the Archetypal tailor, the "self"-intoxicated Dope, Narcissus—the Sleep of heart in here and now.

Let Orpheus be Emperor of all of art and culture's Lighted Happen in your briefest time on here.

Narcissus is the forever dead you should not want or imitate alive.

Behold the Right and Perfect Emperor of all true art and life—the Orphic Icon that is heart itself—that makes the free and ancient culturing of virtue's humankind in mortal time of Realest Light.

Forget the tailor's irony—the path and walk of heartless mirroring of "as-it-were"—and let the fool Narcissus go where Disapparent is, that cannot walk and rule the streets of Where you Are.

XXV.

Aesthetic Ecstasy: Art Without A Mediator

Adi Da Samraj working on *Geome One: Alberti's Window*.

1.

One of the doctrines proclaimed by some influential artists and art critics of the "modern" period is that visual art is "surface-alone"—without any "objective" references, and also without a "subjective" domain in which to exist. According to this paradigm, visual art is merely a "thing" in physical space—and there is no way to enter into it as a meaning-space. Thus, visual art is presumed to be meaningless space—space reduced to meaninglessness, to mere "thing"-ness, to an "objectified" state that has no greater domain in which to exist, or (otherwise) in which to include the perceiver.

This is a "dead-end" understanding of visual art, and of how visual art functions, and of the space within which visual art functions.

Some of the artists who espouse the "surface-alone" paradigm relative to visual art create images in the manner of geometric abstraction. However, the fact that some makers of geometric abstractionist images regard their images to be devoid of "meaning" or "content" does not at all mean that meaninglessness is an inherent quality of all art in the geometric abstractionist mode.

Much of the image-art I make and do—for example, the work I have entitled *Alberti's Window I*—can be legitimately described as being in the mode of geometric abstraction. However, not even any of the most purely geometrically abstractionist examples of the image-art I make and do is a "surface-only" space, or a surface-play of geometricism in and of itself. Indeed, as I have indicated by means of the title *Alberti's Window I*, that image (as one representative among all of the geometrically abstract images I make and do) embodies a disposition that transcends both the "new" view of image-art as "surface-only" and the "old" view (first formulated by Leon Battista Alberti in the fifteenth century) of the image as a perspectivally-organized "window on the world".

If viewers in a museum or gallery of visual art see a number of geometric abstractionist works, by different artists, hanging on the walls, they will tend to see every image primarily in terms of the "shared style"—which, in that case, is the use of organized geometric shapes. Such is how people, in general, are now acculturated to view and understand works of image-art. However, to view works of image-art merely in the context of "art history" and "shared style" is a kind of reductionism. To define and limit works of image-art that are made in the mode of geometric abstraction by references to "art history" and "shared style" alone is to view such images as if there is no meaning conveyed by geometrically precise forms (as opposed to naturalistic forms), and as if all geometrically precise forms are fundamentally "the same thing" simply by virtue of their geometric precision.

There is now a prevailing tendency to view image-art rather exclusively from the perspective of the art historian. From this perspective, every work of image-art is a representation-in-time that can be linked up with other kinds of images that are (likewise) representations-in-time. The art-historical approach creates a systematic overview by seeing everything in terms of the history of academically defined artistic movements. Thus, the meaning of any particular work of image-art tends to be reduced to understanding the "position" of the particular image (and of the artist) in the scheme of historical (and, altogether, academic) accounting.

The art-historical approach to the viewing of image-art is one of the conventions of cultural "ownership" of image-art, which understands (and, effectively, controls and "owns") image-art by categorizing and defining it in terms of historical movements—just as the "art market" categorizes and defines works of image-art in terms of their monetary value as cultural "commodities".

There is, on the one hand, the inherently participatory process of making image-art, and, on the other hand, there is the rather analytical (and, potentially, even dissociative) process of describing (and, thereby, "objectifying") and interpreting image-art. Generally speaking, everyone who looks at a work of image-art is involved (to one or another degree) in the descriptive interpretation of the image as "object"—and, in that process, the straightforward experience of perceptual (and total psycho-physical) participation in the image gets lost in the "objectified" event.

Thus, someone viewing *Alberti's Window I* may respond to it merely as an "example" of geometric abstractionism, an "example" that instantly reminds the individual of images made by other artists who work in the geometric abstractionist mode. By viewing *Alberti's Window I* in this art-historical manner, I, along with even all artists who make and do images in the geometric abstractionist mode, am eased into a convenient position in the historical sequence of academically defined space and time. Such a manner of viewing image-art is, ultimately, a choice to "objectify", control, and be indifferent toward the perceptually-based opportunity of profundity that image-art is. Indeed, if such a choice is made relative to works of image-art, it is (thus) indicated that the same choice otherwise characterizes the "point of view" toward life (and Reality Itself) that is being lived by the viewer.

That being the case, it should be clear that all right and true image-art is tacitly (if not explicitly) purposed to move every viewer beyond the limits of all mere "objectification". That is to say, the fundamental issue inherent in the making and doing of image-art is not the question of whether or not the image should "represent objects" beyond its own surface—but, rather, it is the question of how to draw the viewer beyond the ego-based habit of merely "objectifying" (and analyzing and conceptualizing) the any image that is seen (or even the any perceptual process that is experienced).

To take another example: In a period such as the Renaissance, when realistic representation of the human figure was the principal "subject" matter of virtually all artists, what is the difference between one artist and the next? Botticelli, Leonardo da Vinci, Michelangelo, and Raphael are similar in the sense of the fundamental visual reference to the realistically portrayed human figure—but, in terms of aesthetic force and meaning, each one's art is very distinct from the art of the others.

In any case, comparisons are not a right basis for rightly and truly making use of the perceptual opportunity that is always present in the form of any right and true work of image-art. Primarily and fundamentally, the viewer's free (and unguarded) perceptual (and total psycho-physical) participation is what the process of viewing art should be about—rather than any theoretically-based effort of categorizing, "objectifying", reducing, or comparing.

The ultimate liability of art-historical criticism is represented by the vision of people wandering through museums with earpieces installed, always waiting to hear what the tape-recorded "expert" has to say. When people feel they have to have someone "between" them and the artistic image, explaining what the any image means and where it fits into art history, the scholar and the critic become the necessary mediators of the experience of image-art. When the mediator has become not only valuable but also necessary, and even primary, then, whenever (in the face of an artistic image) people do not have access to a mediator's explanations, they tend to presume and feel that they have no inherent ability to relate to the image-art in front of their eyes. In that case, image-art has become subordinate to the culture of explanation.

Rightly, people should, as an always first principle, freely (perceptually and totally) participate in the viewing of image-art without any association with mere ideas (or disembodied talk), comparisons, "objectifications", reductionism, and academic analysis—or, in other words, entirely without the medium of something-in-between. In the primal moment of free participatory perception, there is no intrinsic mediator—neither the mediator as "other" nor the mediator as "self".

Art critics and art historians obviously have an outstandingly important discriminative and educational function within the larger culture of all image-art—but, fundamentally and ultimately, the image stands, just as it is, in front of (or even all around) the viewer. A work of image-art is never <u>merely</u> "objective", never merely a "thing" on a wall or in an exhibition space. No matter what the stated disposition of anyone (including the artist) may be, a work of image-art, in fact, functions as a "subjective" space of participation for any viewer who directly experiences it.

Thus, I look for all those viewing the image-art I make and do to fully participate in the moment of direct perceptual and total psycho-physical awareness of the any image—without any other references. To participate thus in the viewing of a work of image-art has nothing to do with analytical comparisons and the superimposition of talk and mere ideas. It is simply a matter of unmediated (and intrinsically egoless) participation.

Much contemporary use of image-art is basically about non-participation. It is about the image being "objectified" to the point where no participation is possible other than acknowledging the idea of its "thing"-ness. That is not the right and true approach to the image-art I make and do. I call for right, true, and free participation—not non-participation. I call for fundamental non-"objectification", non-dissociation, and non-mediation.

My image-art functions entirely in the context of perceptually-based whole bodily (or total psycho-physical) participation. My image-art has no political purpose or function. My image-art does not, itself (or by intention), represent any system of academic comparisons and historical accounting. My image-art does not represent any particular doctrine or method that can be said to be "official".

My image-art is the "subjective" space of participation for whoever participates in it. My image-art, most fundamentally, and most essentially, becomes (and, thus, is) the participatory viewer—or the responsive participatory event of the immediate and total psycho-physical activity of viewing the image itself.

I am calling for a right and true use of the image-art I make and do—a use to which even all art should be put—in which the viewer is simply face to face with the art, without anything or anyone in-between, and with no extra-artistic uses whatsoever. Any true moment of participation in a work of art is—in the most positive sense of the word—"use-less", for the viewer. Right and true image-art has no conventional uses. In the case of right and true image-art, there is only the moment in which the viewer fully participates. Right and true image-art is not merely a "thing"-ness on the wall or in the exhibition space. A work of right and true image-art is coincident with (and not in any sense separate or different from) the Intrinsically Self-Evident (and Intrinsically egoless) "Space" That Is Reality Itself—the tacitly present image-space in which the viewer (in present time) is freely participating, without mediation by "self" or "other".

Thus, the primary use of the image-art I make and do is the direct, unmediated moment of participatory perception—for each individual viewer. Just that, now and forever—without making any comparisons between whatever image is being viewed in the moment and any other image or "object" that has ever been seen. The primary use of the image-art I make and do is always in the present moment, and (thus) in the all-transcending moment of Reality Itself—rather than the moment in the space-time-bound context of variations on the human egoic "self"-image. The Reality-moment is the actual moment of free perceptual participation—not the space-time-bound event (or "thing") of non-participation. When rightly viewed, the images I make and do spontaneously become happenings in the egoless "Space" That Is Reality Itself.

Regardless of what any artist may say to "objectify" his or her image-art, the actual happening is still the perceiver in the moment of approaching the image. Free participation in image-art is what people spontaneously do—unless they are prevented from doing so. Currently, the indirect (or socially acculturated, and participation-preventing) uses of image-art are, in general, dominating people's understanding of what is allowable relative to approaching a work of image-art. Indeed, it seems that people, in general, have become accustomed to simply "walking by" the images they go to see. In general, people spend very little time with the works of image-art they go to see (or otherwise look at). At most, they may check the title and the name of the artist—and then they may check to see how it corresponds to the accounts of art history they have been taught. An "objectifying" glance is all that is given to the image itself. If that is the extent of a person's participation in image-art, then the image-art has no right, true, and profound use.

The primary (or directly participatory) use of image-art is, at the present time, being suppressed (or at least avoided) by the many secondary and indirect uses of image-art, such that people can no longer see what is in front of their eyes. If people go to a museum or gallery of visual art and see an image on the wall that they know is worth many millions of dollars, that financial fact tends to be fundamental to how they view the image. Thus, they are experiencing the image as "fame" and "money". They cannot rightly, truly, and profoundly perceive the image itself. They cannot give themselves to the image. They cannot surrender into the process of free participation in the image. They cannot be the happening of the image. They cannot coincide with the image—or its meaning-context in the unmediated instant of their feeling-perception.

The various modes of social and cultural communication about image-art common in the world today tend to dull (or even prevent) people's free perceptual (and even total psycho-physical) participation in artistic images. If you are talking about an artistic image—even if what you say is valid, your experience of the image is not fundamental, primary, participatory, and in the present moment.

What is the primary use of image-art? The primary use of image-art is perceptual (and total psycho-physical) feeling-participation in the totality of the meaning-space that the image-art is. Indeed, that is why image-art should be made. Image-art should and must be made, because it (potentially) enables human beings to participate in human existence (and in Reality Itself) in a right, true, and (potentially) profound sense. If image-art (or even any form or mode of art) does not enable people to participate in human existence (and in Reality Itself) in a right, true, and profound manner, then image-art (or even all art) is merely a minor and relatively meaningless human event.

The primary use of image-art must always be vigorously advocated in the human world. Such advocacy makes it possible for people to feel free to participate in works of image-art, and (thus) to be moved into the meaning-space of image-art, and to thus and thereby be benefited and even transformed by that participation. In the current cultural environment, people need to feel they have permission to take image-art seriously. They need to be told that the image-art they are looking at is serious art, important art, and even great art, before they will even give it the extra moments of glancing that people pay to image-art they feel is significant.

It is unfortunate that people require permission to take image-art seriously—but that is the current cultural situation.

I invite everyone to directly participate in the image-art I make and do—with the understanding that such participation is, primarily and fundamentally, what the images I make and do are about. The various other possible modes of approaching or valuing the images I make and do have significance and importance in the larger context of human culture and the culture of art itself. Nevertheless, the primary use to be made of the images I make and do is unguarded, full-feeling perceptual (and total psycho-physical) participation—beyond all efforts to make comparisons, and beyond all other (or otherwise political, social, economic, or cultural) uses of image-art.

2.

All visual artists are, fundamentally, working to achieve the same result—which is the making of images and three-dimensional shapes, in one form or another, that are authentically about the "aesthetic experience"—which is perceptual and total psycho-physical participation in "significant form". It does not make any difference what may be the style, the apparent "subject"-content, or the moment in history—the "aesthetic experience" is, primarily and fundamentally, what image-art (and even all art) is about.

There are greater and lesser modes of participation in image-art—and there are many aspects of image-art that can be discussed, in addition to the "aesthetic experience". Nevertheless—primarily, and fundamentally—image-art is the "aesthetic experience". Image-art is the characteristics of form, color, structure, and spatial context—and the human perceiver's meaning-resonation with all of that.

Works of image-art by different artists (or even by the same artist) look different from one another—because every artist has a particular style (and even any number of modes of style), but all image-art (essentially) does the same thing, and is about the same thing, which is the "aesthetic experience" itself.

Therefore, there really is no evolution of image-art—nor is comparison of different works of image-art to each other a fundamental occupation. Comparison has its own interest, of course—but it is not primary and fundamental. What is primary and fundamental is the direct perceptual (and total psycho-physical) experience, the intrinsically meaningful "aesthetic experience" of "significant form".

Image-art is not about mere "objectification", as some would like to suggest. Nor is image-art about some kind of ideal view of the world, as some others would say. Primarily and fundamentally, image-art is simply the "aesthetic experience" itself—how form and color, line and structure, come together in the moment of the viewer's intrinsically (and even intensively and inevitably) meaning-making participation in the work of image-art, and how the various aesthetic elements combine with the brain and the nervous system and the whole field of human psycho-physical participation.

All image-art is about this same thing. Either the any particular image is profound in these terms, or it is not. And whether or not the any particular image is profound, there is, nevertheless and irreducibly, the perceiver. Either the perceiver participates profoundly—or not. Therefore, it is that combination of image-art well-made and image-art well-participated-in that makes the moment of direct perception the measure of the "aesthetic experience".

It does not make any primary and fundamental difference how, for instance, Mondrian's style is different from Picasso's style (or anybody else's style). When one is standing in front of an image by anyone at all, the direct moment is about the "aesthetic experience", no matter who made it, and no matter who one is. It is all to be measured by how one participates in the "aesthetic experience" and how well the artist enabled one to participate in the "aesthetic experience".

There are fundamental laws associated with the brain and nervous system, and with the totality of the Real in which human beings participate. Those laws—along with how much free energy and attention the individual perceiver brings to the viewing of image-art—determine whether any example of image-art is actually right and true image-art, and (altogether) how "good" it is. If the viewer brings only a modest capability to perceive the image-art or participate in it, then that is all the viewer gets.

The more someone is free to fully participate in the image-art, and the better the image-art is, then the more profound the viewer's participation will be, and the more profound his or her "aesthetic experience" will be.

Ultimately, right and true image-art is nothing other than Reality Itself. The more that one's participation in a work of image-art coincides with the egoless nature of Reality Itself, the more one's participation in the image-art will be ecstatic.

The "aesthetic experience" is, primarily and fundamentally, about ecstasy—or the experiential transcending of the psycho-physical limits of egoity (or of "self"-separateness).

When the viewing of image-art is right and true, there is a thrill in the event, a profundity of experience—a participatory "Realization" of a state that coincides with the intrinsic unity and integrity of "significant form". If the viewing of image-art is not right and true, then that thrill, that profundity, is absent, and the secondary uses of the image-art come to the fore. Those secondary uses tend to be made primary by the conventions of ordinary (political, social, economic, and cultural) human influence.

The human entity is a living system of psycho-physical integrity, which—like all other integrated natural systems (or pattern-forms of life-process)—is inherently and intrinsically self-organizing, self-correcting, self-rightening, and (ultimately) "self"-transcending. Thus, unless the inherently self-organizing, self-correcting, and self-rightening process of human life is (by any particular means) obstructed and dis-integrated, the human entity will inevitably move into the attitude and state that is "self"-transcending—or ecstatic.

Ecstasy is the primary and fundamental human motive and event. Ecstasy is undeniable participation in the state of prior unity. The transcending of "objectification"—whether of "self" or "world" or Reality Itself—is the primary and fundamental characteristic of right and true human purpose. Therefore, the primary and fundamental purpose of right and true art is aesthetic ecstasy—wherein and whereby the human being is served toward the primary and fundamental human purpose and event that is ecstasy itself (or egoless participation in Reality Itself).

I call people to primary and fundamental participation in the image-art I make and do—which primary and fundamental participation is about the "aesthetic experience", aesthetic ecstasy, and the profundity of egoless participation in Reality Itself. The ecstasy of the viewer is what I would enable (through aesthetic means) by making artistic images. The primary use of image-art is aesthetic ecstasy—therefore, that ecstasy is fundamental to the image-art I make and do.

When people listen to music, there is a mode of whole bodily participation that is, by convention, expected and accepted. People close their eyes, or sway with the music. They pass into a concentrated feeling-space, in which they are not merely looking around the room while they remain detached from the music and bodily oblivious to its effects. When people listen to music, they bodily feel and feelingly respond to it. They are, by means of every kind of political, social, economic, and cultural education, prepared and permitted to do that. There is a conventional culture for such participation in music. Some forms of music are in a "refined" mode and others in a "grosser" mode—but, in any and every case, people tend to participate in music both rhythmically and inwardly. In other words, the conventional culture associated with music remains, even now, associated with the general primary and fundamental human culture of ecstasy (which includes aesthetic ecstasy, or ecstasy served by artistic means).

However, the kind of conventional culture that exists relative to music tends, generally speaking, to be absent in the present-day conventional culture of the visual arts. The visual arts have, to a large degree, lost association with the culture of ecstasy. There has been a reductionist limiting of people's participation in the visual arts—because visual art has become almost entirely "objectified" and "owned" by conventional (and non-ecstatic) political, social, economic, and cultural forces in the common world of "gross realism".

When people go to a museum or gallery of visual art, they generally do not demonstrate the body-language of full feeling-participation that they otherwise manifest in a concert hall. Instead, people in a museum or gallery of visual art are, generally, merely thinking—checking the nameplates, thinking and talking about explanations. They presume that they cannot quite understand what is in front of their eyes, and that (therefore) their viewing of the artistic images must be mediated (and they themselves must be defended from their vulnerability to the images) by explanations (and even by emotionally reactive utterances). In contrast, when people go to a musical performance, they "get with it", readily entering into the space of whole bodily feeling-participation.

Why is it not the case that people go into a museum or gallery of visual art and start swooning in the image-art? Why are visitors to a museum or gallery of visual art characteristically unable to "get with it"?

"Getting with it" is, primarily and fundamentally, what image-art is about. Instead of treating image-art as some kind of an "opponent" (or even a "deceiver") that requires a mediator in-between to protect the viewer from it, to "distance" the viewer from it, to give the viewer an "angle", an advantage on it, a power over it, people should dare to "get with it", and (thus) freely enter into the ecstasy of disarmed participation.

When the images I make and do are exhibited under the best of circumstances, an intentionally set-apart space is created, wherein people are tacitly given the freedom to enter into ecstasy. The freedom to enter into ecstasy (by aesthetic means) is not generally the case in the present-day domain of the visual arts—but it should be.

The ecstasy of the "aesthetic experience" should be the primary and fundamental mode of participation in <u>all</u> art. Art is a dimension of human culture whereby people are enabled to enter into ecstasy—potentially transcending even some of the daily limitations and dramatizations of egoity, and certainly transcending the limits of merely social conformity.

Much bad image-art is merely about conforming people to the programs of social and political indoctrination. I view much of the image-art of the present day to be just that. It is, essentially, political art. It indoctrinates people and limits people to social and political programs—and, therefore, to social-ego, or political-ego, confinement. Thus, it is not profoundly different from the programmed image-art of totalitarian regimes, the official "realism" of the state, and so forth.

Such image-art enforces a view of life that is anti-ecstatic—and that is what I am criticizing about it. Such image-art does not permit the "aesthetic experience". It is opposed to the "aesthetic experience". It is about the corruption of the "aesthetic experience", the destruction of it. It suppresses ecstasy. That is what is wrong with it.

The art-historical approach to the viewing of image-art is part of the armoring associated with image-art in museums, galleries, and in the public marketplace altogether. Visual art has been put into a circumstance in which people do not participate in it to the point of ecstasy—whereas vocal music, instrumental music, dance, and various other auditory arts still exist in a field of ecstatic participation. This non-ecstatic limiting of the experience of visual art is obviously not right and should be corrected. The spaces within which image-art is made, and (otherwise) viewed, should be places of humanly-realized ecstasy.

The freedom to enter into ecstasy is not something that is accounted for, generally speaking, in the museum and gallery spaces of the visual arts of the present day. Instead, there are various kinds of limits, restrictions, and prohibitions relative to "how to view" the image-art and the sculptural art. And a primary prohibition is the presumed necessity of talk, or the mediator-explainer—or explanation itself.

My images are large by intention—for all kinds of reasons. The monumental size calls for full physical participation, such that the viewer is drawn into a space that is beyond his or her ability to contain and limit the images by means of explanations or by means of any physical activity. My images call for ecstasy. They enable ecstasy—the ecstasy that is indigenous to the "aesthetic experience".

The image-art I make and do (and, also, the literary art I make and do*) is, primarily and fundamentally, about "significant form", aesthetic ecstasy, and ecstasy itself—and (ultimately) the ego-transcending Realization of Reality Itself.

* Adi Da's "literary art" includes his trilogy entitled *The Orpheum* (comprising *The Mummery Book*, *The Scapegoat Book*, and *The Happenine Book*), as well as his poems collected in *Crazy Da Must Sing*.

XXVI.

My Material Art Must Forever Remain Within The Perfect Room

I have made many tens of thousands of images, and I intend (if all allows) to make numberless more. Very few of the images I have yet made have been (originally) hand-fashioned. Most of the images I have made have yet to be materially fabricated. The act of materially fabricating the images I make requires, first of all, a (generally, public) process of appreciatively responsive and financially-backed acquisition and exhibition. Therefore, the material fabricating of the image-art I make is always subsequent to the original making of the image-compositions themselves.

Even if any particular image I have made becomes materially fabricated by means of appreciatively responsive and financially-backed acquisition and exhibition, I have also made tens of thousands of images more—and I will (if time and all enabling allows) make even many tens of thousands more and more. Therefore, not even the most generous and vigorous supporting and enacting of the necessary process of materially fabricating the images I have made and would yet make could possibly bring <u>all</u> the images to actual material fabrication while I am alive—regardless of how many years I might yet remain alive to do the necessary manuality of their happening.

There are many other, and very practical, issues necessarily associated with the material fabricating of any particular image I make. I expect, and it must forever be required, that the material fabricating of the image-art I make always be exactly right and true to the aesthetic characteristics and the meaning-characteristics inherent and particular to the any image being fabricated—and that all the particular and general instructions I give relative to the material fabricating of any particular image be strictly carried out (including the requirement of longest-term durability and longevity, as well as overall fineness of craftsmanship, in every detail). Therefore, the <u>material</u> enactment of any image I make is not only dependent on the response, the appreciation, and the financial support provided by others, but, also, on all the careful manualist craft and necessary technology that must be provided by others in order to make a right and true "incarnation" of what I have made.

Because of the comparatively subtle nature of the medium in which I make images, they exist only in (generally) electronic form and (otherwise) archived modes of artifact that are not yet "material fabrications" that can be acquired and exhibited. And, yet—altogether, definitively, and certainly—I have already and actually made and truly fully completed each and all of the many tens of thousands of images I have made.

If I were to manually enact the material fabricating of the images I make—or even become occupied with all the managerial overseeing required to manufacture exactly right and durable material fabrications of the images I make—I would be required to enter into business and management activities that would not only contradict the inherently and formally renunciate characteristics of the life I live, but would (otherwise) profoundly limit (and even interfere with) the prolific image-making process with which I am otherwise profoundly and constantly engaged.

The manualism of image-manufacture is, actually, an aspect of art business—which, altogether, necessitates material occupation, management activities, and (even as a prerequisite) the promoting and selling of the materially-fabricated works. I have chosen a mode of artistic activity that does not, itself, require any business activities, any relinquishment of the context of formal renunciation, or even any manual endeavor (outside the physical activity inherent in the original image-making itself). Therefore, I can and must freely leave all aspects of the material fabricating of the images I make to be managed and enacted by others—although I call for all of that (along with all responsibility for the business of promoting and selling the materially-fabricated works) to be done by fully skilled, responsively enthusiastic, and exactly careful professionals.

Relative to the potential material fabricating of the images I make, I always provide full instructions (and while I yet live, active consultation)—but I always stand apart from struggle with the event, the doers, and the business necessarily associated with the material fabricating of the images I make.

I make images. I do not merely "conceive" them. Yet, I do not materially fabricate them—or, otherwise, follow them into the marketplace of material art. I do not disdain, or belittle, or underestimate the necessity and importance of either the manualism or the business necessary to the material domain of image-art—but I do not directly function in a physically active manner within the material, or business, or otherwise open public dimension of image-process.

Thus, I am, and will remain, constantly and always freely concentrated in image-making—but always and only within the sphere and studio of that specific and profound concentration. Nevertheless, I would have even every image I make go on to material fabrication—such that even every one and all may (now, and forever hereafter) participate in the images I make.

Because no particular material fabrication of an image can be perfectly final, permanent, and absolute—any image I make could, in principle, be materially re-fabricated even many times in the totality of future time. And, so, it should be.

I regard the images I make to be "image-compositions"—much like the scores for musical compositions that are the basic works made by the composers of music. Why, then, should the images I make (or, as such, compose) not be allowed to be materially fabricated (and, as such, "performed") even by many material fabricators (or "performers") over time?

The material fabrications of the images I make should all be only (as it were) "licensed manufacturings"—with, perhaps, a formal agreement that further "licenses" will be allowed only after specific and even extended periods of time have elapsed (or, otherwise, only if any further material fabrications that are done sooner are done only in modes of material medium and craft that are significantly different from what was previously and recently done). Therefore, and on this basis, material fabrications of the images I make should always be formally authorized, professionally made, and (when completed) formally approved and certified—but I will not do hand-written signatures upon any such "performed" work (any more than musicians, conductors, actors, or any other artistic performers should be required to bear the hand-written signature of a composer or a playwright in the theatre of performances).

All the image-art I make is done in the "First Room" of effectively solitary contemplation. All "others" must yet find every image also here (therein)—where ego-"I" and "other" have neither place nor time in which to be concealed.

The Space in which material eyes can truly rightly see the image-art I make is also only that "First Room"—wherein Reality Itself Is Only "Perfect Knowledge" As What Is.

XXVII.

In Plain Sight Without A Word

Visual art (or image-art) is, fundamentally, a perceptual happening.

If any example of visual art (or image-art) is, altogether, right and true, it is—inherently, and as a perceptual happening—full of perceptually-encoded (and perceptually-concretized) meaning, conveyed via the perceptual laws that are intrinsically associated with (and required by) the (necessarily, deeply-"located") "aesthetic experience" of "significant form".

Therefore, right and true visual art (or image-art) requires fullest perceptual participation and fullest perceptually-based participatory responsiveness—all of which is, fundamentally, a tacit (or non-conceptual) process, which happens (experientially) in the aesthetic deep-domain (of bodily energies, emotional feeling-awareness, and brain-and-nervous-system structures of responsive apprehension), and which (thus and thereby) happens to happen in the Primal Consciousness-Domain of Intrinsically Wordless Reality Itself.

The making of visual art (or image-art) that is both right and true is, fundamentally (and in its depth), done in silence and (effectively) in solitude.

Likewise, right and true participatory viewing (or seeing) of right and true visual art (or image-art) is, fundamentally (and in its depth), done in silence and (effectively) in solitude.

Therefore, if there is more to be said about a particular example of visual art (or image-art) than there is to see about it—either the artist has not achieved right and true participatory perceptual art in that particular case or the viewer has not achieved right and true participation in the particular event of approaching it.

Indeed, if visual art (or image-art) is, in general, more talked about than seen (in the full participation-responsive perceptual and aesthetic manner), the culture associated with the doing and the using of visual art (or image-art) is, itself, in need of a profound—and even "radical" (or "at-the-root")—reformation.

Right and true visual art (or image-art) is, fundamentally (and in its depth), not a social event, or a sociopolitical phenomenon.

Right and true visual art (or image-art) should, most rightly and truly, be visited in silence, in depth, and in a context of deepest aloneness (even if in public places).

Right and true visual art (or image-art) is wordless silence—concretized by a perceptually-based form that is as if spontaneously appearing, and standing in plain sight without even a single word of explanation.

Right and true visual art (or image-art) speaks to silence, in silence—or by silent, non-discursive, unexplained, and tacitly-to-be-received means.

To speak—and, altogether, to explain—in the circumstance of what should be deep-participation in the perceptible aesthetic presence of a work of right and true visual art (or image-art) is a kind of subordination of what is sacred (or of deepest "location") to what is profane (or of merely "outward", and, altogether, merely social, significance and use).

This is not to say that speaking about works of right and true visual art (or image-art)—or even attempting to explain them—is never appropriate.

However, speech and explanation in reference to right and true visual art (or image-art) are not appropriate if they are made a substitute for (or, otherwise, an obstruction to) right and true perceptual-aesthetic participation and in-depth participatory responsiveness, or if speech and explanation overly (or even merely) "objectify" (and, thereby, dissociate the viewer from) works of right and true visual art (or image-art), or if speech and explanation reduce the art and the experience of the art to a superficial, depthless, gross, and talkative stimulation of otherwise detached, non-participatory, merely analytical, and (altogether) unresponsive habit-patterns of body and mind.

In art, as in life altogether, what the perceiver sees (or, in any manner, experiences) is limited only by the degree to which egoity (or the "self"-contraction of the complex body-mind) is not transcended in unguarded participatory surrender into the intrinsically wordless (or tacit) process of the seeing (or the experiencing) itself.

What the perceiver sees is whatever of Reality Itself the perceiver is willing and able to allow to Be—and (Thus and Thereby) to Be (and to Be seen) in plain sight.

Right and true visual art (or image-art) is a primary human (and humanizing) means whereby right and true seeing is both enacted (in the case of the artist) and enabled (in the case of the viewer)—and even such that Reality Itself (Which Is Truth Itself, and The Beautiful Itself) may Be allowed to Be seen in plain sight without a word.

True silence—including the intrinsic silence of right and true visual art (or image-art)—intrinsically and unguardedly allows all of Reality Itself to Be.

What Is seen—when seeing is right and true—Is Reality Itself.

XXVIII.

The Authentic Artistic Discipline of Truth Itself, Beauty Itself, and Reality Itself

Anciently, all arts were forms of ritual. The arts have always served the culture of traditional society. In the traditional (and, now, much less prevalent) setting, there were composers, musicians, singers, dancers, painters, sculptors, people who wrote poems and stories, and people who would recite—but the artists did not engage their forms of art merely as a means of expressing themselves. Traditional artists engaged their art forms with the understanding that the arts had a sacred function within society. Traditional artists studied and practiced disciplines for years, in order to become proficient in a particular art. If, over a long testing-time, an individual proved himself or herself to have sufficient talent and ability in a particular art, his or her entire life would be devoted to the making and doing of that particular form of art.

In general, the practicing culture of any traditional society was—and, insofar as such traditions are still maintained (in some tradition-based societies), the traditional practice yet remains—a matter of participation in a pre-established pattern and process. Each traditional culture had a prescribed formula, a philosophy, a history. Every traditional culture had parameters within which an individual could operate as an artist. As a painter, for example, the technique one was to use and the images one was to create were all prescribed by tradition. Therefore, the artist had to transcend himself or herself in order to learn and practice the art the tradition required. In order to accomplish this, the traditional artist submitted (and, even now, submits) himself or herself to a master of his or her craft or art, by whom the artist would be schooled in the established culture—in other words, in the tradition, the limits, the techniques, and the purposes of the art. By submitting himself or herself to such traditional requirements, the artist would discipline and transcend his or her own ego-based or independent motivations.

The traditional artist was always required to learn his or her art under strict guidance and supervision, and was not permitted to paint or perform music or engage in any other art form without such supervision until the master could attest to the artist's preparation and affirm that he or she was capable of serving the culture in the traditional manner. The traditional artist would be capable of this service not only because he or she had learned all the techniques, and not only because he or she knew how to awaken in the audience all the traditional artistic (and, generally, mythological, legendary, and iconic) modes of idea and form to which the people were (by tradition) devoted and by which they might (it was believed) transcend themselves, but the traditional artist would have also (and first of all) mastered himself or herself in the process of becoming such a servant of the tradition. The traditional artist always and first of all had to become truly responsible for himself or herself before he or she could be permitted to practice any art within his or her cultural tradition.

In modern (or less and less tradition-based) times, the arts have gradually (and, now, virtually finally) ceased to have a cultural purpose that is acknowledged to be necessary (or even necessarily positive, auspicious, counter-egoic, and most profound). As a result, the arts have, in most places and circumstances, become mere public and private entertainments—or merely secular (or non-sacred, and entirely ego-serving and ego-bound) diversions and absurdities. The arts have become methods for expressing the contents, or the "insides", of the ego-"self"—or of dramatizing personal aberrations and ironies. In fact, the arts have become principal (and, generally, "social realist") means for expressing the problems that people have because of the fact that there is no culture, no center, no society, no necessity to what people do—and no culturally-honored and intensively prescribed and implemented way out of the vicious circle of egoity (or "Narcissus") itself. Therefore, what artists (in general) presently represent—as artists and as human beings—is the failure of the social order, the collapse of civilizing tradition, the disappearance of the cultural demand that artists transcend themselves, that they be first mastered in order to master themselves, that they provide something within the social order that is culturally valuable and deeply beneficial to others, or an art that has intrinsic value, that has fundamental ("root and branch") value, that is not just decorative or entertaining or diverting or merely grossly stimulating, but that is part of the sacred and highest purposes of a right and true human culture.

Because of the present-day situation of global secularization, and the collapse of civilization in general, and the disappearance of sacred culture in particular, it is profoundly necessary that all who aspire to artistic practice must now re-discover how to submit themselves to the right and true function of art within a setting of right and true (and, in the future, necessarily global) human culture. That is how artists will (by right practice) transcend themselves within an authentic artistic process and (thus and thereby) make their art more than mere ego-dramatization, or absurd "self"-expression, or mere Narcissistic "self"-reflection, and the awful transmission of benighted human "end-products" to the always already suffering world of humanity.

True artists must (now, as ever before) endure the discovery-discipline wherein art can be authentically ecstatic (or truly ego-transcending and Ultimate-Reality-Revealing)—and they must, also, endure the process of discovering how (as a result) their art can (now, and in the future) profoundly serve the global culture in which all must live. It is only through true ecstasy-discipline that artists can find a way to communicate the necessary "essence" and "significant form" of Truth Itself, Beauty Itself, and Reality Itself through their art, and have that communication serve the ecstatic mood of participation in Truth Itself, Beauty Itself, and Reality Itself in the audiences and patrons of their art.

Ultimately, the right and true role of artists is to discover and practice a higher and truly great purpose in their art—by discovering how their art can be ecstatic, even in the Spiritual (although not necessarily religious) sense, and how their art can serve intrinsically (and necessarily) egoless participation in Truth Itself, Beauty Itself, and Reality Itself, even in all who attend it. That purpose requires a profoundly ego-transcending discipline as a basis for right and true art-practice.

Inevitably, it will take a lifetime to accomplish the egoless ecstatic practice of right and true art—and the actual accomplishment may only rarely, and in the case of rare individuals, be truly great, truly culture-changing, and life-transforming for all, and able to endure for longest and even forever time. Nevertheless, the right and true artistic struggle is not purposed merely to fulfill oneself and make that "self" lovable by the world. The right and true artistic struggle is to transcend oneself, in order to be entered fully into the Truth, the Beauty, and the Reality That Is beyond "self". If that right and true artistic struggle is fully embraced in a truly ego-forgetting and ecstatic manner, free of all the irony of "difference" that ego otherwise makes and does, then the art that is made and done will authenticate and prove itself—by its intrinsic and great and ecstasy-transmitting power to awaken and change all who receive its works.

XXIX.

The ego-Transcending Ordeal of Making Right and True Art

The common principal "subject" of the current "average" of art is the "total world" (as a chaos of material events and "gross realities").

Truly, at any other time or period in the human (and would-be-"humanizing") culture of art-making, the "total world" (as a chaos of material events and "gross realities") could have been embraced as the common principal "subject"—but that actual choice was not made the "average" of art until very recently (and even "post-modernly").

The "total world" is (inherently) a chaos of material events and "gross realities"—because the "world", as a totality, is an always yet dis-orderly (or not-yet-perfected-and-finalized) process of present (and always impending) changes, happening in the inherently imperfect context of "everything-all-at-once".

Truly, it is only as a result and characteristic of twentieth-century (and, now, twenty-first-century) human developments that it has even become possible to (literally) view and (face-to-face) participate in the total chaos of world-events and the daily "gross"-picture of "objectified" humanity.

Indeed, as a direct effect of the globalizing media of new technologies, living in the world is now a poor and crowded live-in situation of intimate dormitory with all the human chaos of "gross realities".

The art of the past was made by artists who also (in their own manner and time) "knew" both the chaos and the "gross realities" of life—but they, unlike the typical artists of the present time, characteristically conceived of art as a means for transcending what is (otherwise) merely gross and chaotic.

Therefore, the art of the past did not, in general, make the "total world" of chaos and "gross realities" into the common principal "subject" of art.

People today generally appear to assume that they are, somehow, "obliged" to make the "total world" of chaos and "gross realities" into their intimate home and sphere of life.

The pervasiveness of invasive communications media invades the every intimate domain of ordinary living in the present-day—and, as a result, the "total world" of chaos and "gross realities" has become the presumed "obligatory" context (and the common principal "subject") of almost everyone's daily life.

It would seem, then, that this situation—in which all of daily (and even intimate) life has become subjugated to chaos and "gross reality"—is the "reason" why present-day art has, most typically (or on "average"), chosen the "total world" (or the general chaos of material events and "gross realities") as its common principal "subject".

The procedure (or technical method) of the current "average" of art is that of ego-based mere reflectivity—or the "gross-realism"-method of merely mirroring chaos and "gross reality".

What of either virtue or beauty or illumination can be seen in the dull, and awful, and "self"-deluded mirror and mirroring of what is merely "grossly" and chaotically happening?

What is merely happened in the streets is the entropy and product of the casual "gross" disintegration and "gross" disorder of the "everything-all-at-once".

All of that being the evident ordinary and present-day case, it is, surely, now time to critically review the choices that are currently being made by humankind and by its culture of art and of practicing artists.

The subjugation of humankind—and of art—to the "total world" of chaos and "gross realities" is not necessary, not inevitable, not right, and not a true basis for either life or art.

Therefore—relative to the subjugation of life and art to the "total world" of chaos and "gross realities"—I say No!

Both life and art must be made right and true—by being intrinsically founded (and always firmly purposed) in what is (inherently) right and true.

Right and true life-practice—and the art-practice and art-culture that right and true life creates—are, necessarily, conformed to the disposition and the means that transcend mere chaos and merely "gross realities".

Life and art that are right and true are, necessarily, conformed to the purpose of transcendence—altogether.

Therefore, art that is right and true is, necessarily, profoundly conformed to the characteristics of "significant form" and to the means that are inherent to the "aesthetic experience"—wherein and whereby chaos and mere "gross realities" are transcended by the exercise of specifically artistic (and, thus, aesthetically responsible and aesthetically responsive) principles and means.

The "how" to do right and true art (and the choosing of the right, and true, and intrinsically necessary "subject" of right and true art) is a profound creative "consideration", which can be resolved only by the artist's own most intense and life-long confrontation with the "total world" of chaos and mere "gross realities"—and most fundamentally, by the artist's own most intense and life-long confrontation with the chaos, the "gross realities", the illusions, the falseness, and (altogether) the egoity of the artist's own presumed and suffered "self".

Therefore, the "total world"—or the inherently chaotic "gross realities" of egoic and not-transcended human experience—is not, in and of itself, the right and true "subject" of right and true art.

The "gross realism" that reflects and indulges in mere convention and "world"-happenstance is neither the characteristic nor the purpose of right and true art.

Right and true art must be the servant, the mirror, and the transmitting-agent of what is (inherently) right and true—or else art is merely an instrument of human ego-bondage and un-illuminated suffering.

Right and true art must illuminate (or serve to En-light-en) the life of the artist and the lives of the rightly and truly participatory perceivers of the art.

Right and true artists are those who endure the necessary ordeal of "self"-discipline and ego-transcending practice (of both life and art), until the artist's own life, and art, and inspiration—rather than the "total world" of otherwise chaotic "gross realities" itself—becomes both right and true.

The "total-world-chaos" of "gross realities" is not, in and of itself, right and true art.

Right and true art cannot "cause" the "total-world-chaos" of "gross realities" to become non-chaotic (or altogether right and true).

Right and true art can (and must) illuminate (or serve to En-light-en) the lives of those who rightly and truly make or use it.

So be it.

XXX.

True Art Always Causes More Art

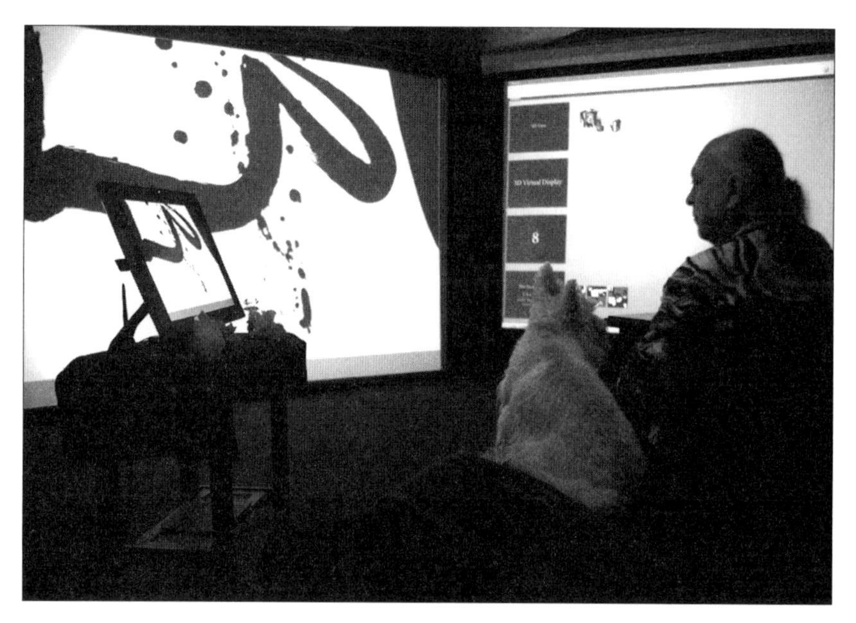

Adi Da Samraj working on *The Struwwelpeter Suite, Part Six.*

True art does not and cannot bring the process of art to an end.

True art makes more art inevitable.

Every work of true art effectively "causes" all future works of true art.

Every work of true art is, effectively, "caused" by all past works of true art.

There is not (and cannot be) a final (or last) work of true art.

Even a perfect work of true art cannot bring the process of art to an end.

Therefore, the effort to defeat (or bring an end to) the urge to make and do more art is futile—and, likewise, the effort to defeat (or bring an end to) all other art (and even all other artists) is absurd.

True art is neither chess nor dice nor poker.

True art is the Irreducible Beloved—to be "Won" at Infinite and Perfect Cost of "self".

XXXI.

Picture Perfect: A Final Imagery of This

Reality (Itself)
 Is Truth (Itself)
 Is The Beautiful (Itself).

These Three—Reality Itself, Truth Itself, and The Beautiful Itself—Are The Absolutes (and The Perfect Obligations) of all meaning.

These Three Absolutes Are The Mutual and Indivisible Measure of One Another.

These Three Absolutes (Together) Are The One, and Indivisible, and Necessary Measure of all art.

These Three Absolutes (Together) Are The Necessary, Intrinsic, and Inherently Perfect "Subject" of all right and true art.

Reality (Itself) Is Truth (Itself) Is The Beautiful (Itself).

Right and true art egolessly Coincides with Reality (Itself), Truth (Itself), and The Beautiful (Itself).

To rightly and truly make and do right and true art requires ego-surrendering (and even Intrinsically and Perfectly ego-transcending) devotion to Reality (Itself), Truth (Itself), and The Beautiful (Itself).

To rightly and truly make and do right and true art is to be the egoless servant of Reality (Itself), Truth (Itself), and The Beautiful (Itself).

To rightly and truly make and do right and true art requires absolute commitment, unwavering concentration, total life-surrender, boundless generosity, and the utter transcending of the imposition of irony as a characteristic of the act of making and doing art.

The Beautiful Itself Is Reality Itself Is Truth Itself Is

To rightly and truly serve the image-art-Demonstration of Reality (Itself) As Truth (Itself) As The Beautiful (Itself) is to make and do and show and enable the egoless seeing of "significant form"—always in its Perfect Moment, and never a moment before or after That.

XXXII.

What Is No-"point-of-view" Is all-and-All

The Mere and Only Presence.
Mere and Only.
Indivisibly One—and Only.
The Mere Presence.
Reality Only.
Only Reality Itself.
The Mere and Only Presence Of Reality Itself.
Mere and One.
Mere.
One.
Only.
Only all.
Only all-and-All.
That Is.
That Is all.
That Is all-and-All.
Only egoless One.
No "difference".
No "difference" no separateness Is—and Only.
Is As all-and-All As One and Prior Unity Of all-and-All.
All "cause-and-effect" In and Of That Only.
Acausal egoless Only That.
The Presence Of Reality Itself.
No "Deity" Is That Is.
Only God That Is Reality Itself No-Deity Divine.
All of all-and-All Is Only That Is As all-and-All Indivisibly.
No "selves" Are here.
Only opposites, and circles, and cycles, and spin.
Nothing conditionally arises that is not a pattern thus.

Every "problem" is only pattern—and, therefore, only a condition of opposites in a state of mutual contradiction, or irreducible opposition, or internal conflict, or spin.

To seek a "solution" to any "problem" by struggling with its pattern is only to become entangled in the mummery of opposites, by means of egoic "self"-identification with conflict and circularity, which only produces more and more cycles of patterns and "problems".

The only Perfect Resolution to any "problem" Is always At the Root, Prior to the "problem", and Prior to the state of "problem" itself, and Prior to the ego-"I" that "knows" and seeks in the domain of pattern itself.

The only Perfect Resolution to "problem" and the search for "solutions" Is always Prior to ego-"I" and its "object"—or At the Root, or In the Source-Position, and As the Source-Condition In and Of and As Which opposites, and circles, and cycles, and spin, and all-and-All of pattern, and "problem", and search arise.

The world is only patterns, patterning the all-and-All Of Only.

The world is only pattern patterning itself—a self-perpetuating figure of duality, "difference", change, uncertainty, and certain death.

You Are Not In, Of, and As the world.

You Are Always Already—Priorly, and At Root—What Is No-"point-of-view".

What Is No-"point-of-view" Is all-and-All. ■

GLOSSARY

The following are the definitions that Adi Da Samraj intended for terms used in this book.

Adi Da Samraj uses quotation marks around certain terms to indicate that he is not using these terms as they are conventionally understood and used.

Adi Da Samraj capitalizes terms that refer to the Non-conditional State of Reality Itself.

---

abstraction—In reference to his own art, Adi Da Samraj uses the term "abstraction" to indicate the process of responding to the subject of an artwork and revealing its nature beyond "point of view", by presenting the subject in a visually reduced and simplified (or essentialized), and not necessarily recognizable, manner.

aesthetic ecstasy—Adi Da uses the word "ecstasy" to mean "standing (*-stasis*) outside (*ec-*)" of "point of view" (or the presumption of existing as a separate self). Thus, to enjoy "aesthetic ecstasy" is to spontaneously come to rest in the inherently blissful "position" prior to "point of view"—in the context of participating in true art.

Alberti, Leon Battista—Leon Battista Alberti (1404–1472) was, among other things, a Renaissance artist who is known in art historical terms for his view (crucial to the development of perspective during the Renaissance) that the painter's canvas is to function as a "window" to the natural, objective world.

all-and-All—A phrase Adi Da created to describe the totality of conditional existence—both as the "sum of its parts" and as an undivided whole. Lowercase "all" indicates "the collected sum of all presumed-to-be-separate beings, things, and conditions", and uppercase "All" indicates "the All (or the undivided totality) of conditional existence as a whole".

anegoic—Not egoic. Adi Da uses this term to mean "egoless", or "without the presumption of a separate 'point of view'". He also indicates an additional meaning of "not useful to the ego".

aniconic—Not iconic. Adi Da uses this term to mean "not representing a separate 'point of view'".

aperspectival—Not perspectival, or "not constructed in accordance with the established laws of perspective". Adi Da also gives this term the extended meaning of "not constructed so as to support the presumption of a separate 'point of view'".

causal (dimension)—*See* **gross, subtle, causal**.

closed fist / open hand—Adi Da used the closed fist as a metaphor for the activity of the ego (contracting from the field of relations into a separate "point of view"), and the open hand as a sign of the human being in free and participatory relationship to all he or she encounters.

conditionality—*See* **Reality Itself / Reality-Condition**.

Conscious Light—In defining Reality Itself as "Conscious Light", Adi Da Samraj is communicating that the two essential characteristics of Reality are Awareness (or Consciousness) and Radiance (or Light, or Energy). Furthermore, Adi Da states that Conscious Light is the essential Nature of every thing and every being in the universe. *See also* **Reality Itself / Reality-Condition**.

Consciousness-Energy Medium—The true "Substance" of all that appears. In agreement with certain Eastern philosophical traditions, Adi Da Samraj defines Consciousness and Energy as the two fundamental characteristics of the one and indivisible Reality.

"dark" epoch, or "late-time"—Adi Da uses these terms to describe the present era—in which doubt of anything beyond mortal existence pervades the entire world, and self-interest is regarded to be the ultimate principle of life.

depth / in-depth—Terms used by Adi Da to indicate the domain of human awareness and experience that lies beyond conventional, superficial, or social exchanges.

"difference"—Adi Da defines "difference"—that is, the presumed "difference" between self and other, self and world, and so forth—as the essential fault that characterizes the human ego. The core of this presumption is the primal notion that "self" is separate (or different) from "everything and everyone else". That primal notion is described by Adi Da as the root of all human suffering and dilemma.

ego / ego-"I" / ego-"self"—Adi Da defines "ego" not as any kind of personal or psychological entity or essence, but, rather, as an activity—the habitual activity of contraction as a separate "self". The largely unconscious activity of self-contraction is the expression of the underlying presumption that "I am separate from everything and everyone else".

As a synonym for "ego", Adi Da often uses compound terms such as "ego-'I'" or "ego-'self'". The quotation marks around "I" and "self" indicate that, in Reality, there is no such thing as the separate "I" (or "self"), even though it is presumed to be the case in ordinary experience.

To be egoless is to exist entirely without the presumption of separation from Reality Itself, or from anything that appears.

ego-art—*See* **Reality-art**.

"First Room"—A poetic reference to the Indivisible Nature of Reality Itself. It is "within" the "First Room" of Reality Itself that all beings and things seem to appear.

Geome—Adi Da's term for the abstract geometric formal element of his image-art, taking the form of squares, circles, and triangles (or rectilinear, curvilinear, and angular shapes).

God-art—*See* **Reality-art**.

gross "realism"—A reduction of the True Nature of Reality to nothing but what can be perceived and experienced in merely physical terms. *See also* **Transcendental Realism/Realist**.

gross, subtle, causal—Adi Da Samraj (in agreement with certain esoteric schools of spirituality) describes conditional existence as having three fundamental dimensions—gross, subtle, and causal.

"Gross", in this case, means "made up of material (or physical) elements". The gross dimension is, therefore, associated with the physical body.

The subtle dimension, which pervades and is senior to the gross dimension, consists of the etheric functions (or the dimension of personal life-energy), the lower mental functions (including the conscious mind, the subconscious mind, and the unconscious mind), and higher mental functions (of discriminative mind, mentally presumed egoity, and will).

The causal dimension is senior to both the gross and the subtle dimensions. It is the root-sense of existence as a separate "self".

inner integrity (or root-indivisibility)—The core (or heart) of the human being, in contrast to the outwardly evident behavior patterns or personality traits of an individual. The inner integrity of the human being is not a separate "some-one", like a "soul", but rather that "place" in each person which is resonant with all beings and things, and with Reality Itself, without presuming separate and personal existence.

"knowing" / "knowledge" / "known"—Adi Da places these words in quotation marks to indicate that the ego's characteristic presumption of separation between the "knower" and that which is "known" makes it impossible to "know" anything as it really is.

"late-time"—*See* **"dark" epoch, or "late-time"**.

Linead—Adi Da's term for his freehand line drawings or brush paintings that are fundamental elements of his "fully resolved" image-art.

"locatedness" / "location" / "self-locatedness" / space-time-"locatedness"—Adi Da places these terms in quotation marks to indicate that "location" is only a presumption of the separate (and illusory) "point of view".

Love-Bliss-"Brightness"—The perfect blissfulness of Reality Itself—a blissfulness that is beyond any potential physical, emotional, mental, psychic, or mystical experience.

maya—A traditional Sanskrit term for the illusory nature of the world.

mummery theatre—The dictionary defines "mummery" as "a ridiculous, hypocritical or pretentious ceremony, observance, or performance". Adi Da uses the term "mummery" to describe the activities of ego-bound beings, who are committed to the false view of separation and separativeness.

"Narcissus"—Adi Da uses "Narcissus" as a key symbol of the un-enlightened individual as a seeker, obsessively enamored of his or her own "self"-image and egoic "self"-consciousness.

He is the ancient one visible in the Greek myth, who was the universally adored child of the gods, who rejected the loved-one and every form of love and relationship, and who was finally condemned to the contemplation of his own image—until, as a result of his own act and obstinacy, he suffered the fate of eternal separateness and died in infinite solitude.

—Adi Da Samraj
The Knee of Listening

Non-conditional—Not dependent on conditions. *See* **Reality Itself / Reality-Condition**.

non-"objective"—*See* **"object" / "objectify" / "objective" / non-"objective"**.

non-"subjective"—*See* **"subject" / "subjective" / non-"subjective"**.

"object" / "objectify" / "objective" / non-"objective"—Adi Da places these terms in quotation marks, in order to indicate that, in Reality Itself, there is no such thing as an "object" that is separate from the "subject".

Therefore, when Adi Da Samraj describes his art as "non-'objective'", he is not saying that his images are entirely devoid of recognizable elements, or are entirely "abstract" (in the commonly used sense of that term). Rather, by referring to his art as "non-'objective'", he is indicating that he intends his art to communicate the True Condition of Reality—in which there are no separate objects, because there is no separation between any apparent object and any apparent subject.

Orphic Font—A "substitute alphabet" of Linead forms, used by Adi Da Samraj as a technical device for image-making (as described in his essay "The Final Resolution of Geome, Linead, and Orphic Font").

"Perfect Knowledge"—The direct Realization of the Indivisible Unity of Reality Itself—prior to any presumption of separation between "knower" and "known". "Perfect Knowledge" contrasts with all forms of ordinary "knowledge"—which are based on the presumption of an irreducible separation between "knower" and "known", or "subject" and "object".

Perfectly Subjective—Adi Da uses this phrase to describe Reality Itself as "Subject", as opposed to being an objective "Other". "Subjective" does not have the meaning of "relating to the inward experience of an individual", but, rather, it means "Being Reality Itself, the True 'Subject' of all apparent experience".

performance-assisted "subjective" process—A phrase Adi Da uses for the process of participation in his art and his theatrical works, which indicates that each individual goes through his or her own inward (or subjective) course of response to the performance or artwork presented. The performance or artwork is not intended to be an objectified thing, but rather an assistance to a transformation of consciousness for the participant.

"point of view"—By placing this phrase in quotation marks, Adi Da is communicating that, in Reality, every "point of view" is an illusion—because all "points of view" are founded in the false presumption of the separate existence of "I".

prior unity—Adi Da's term "prior unity" points to the unity that exists prior to (or beyond) all the apparent differences and conflicts in the world.

psycho-physical—A phrase which Adi Da uses to indicate that the human being is not a purely physical phenomenon, but a phenomenon with both physical and psychological/psychic dimensions. He also uses this description to characterize not only the human being but the world altogether.

"radical"—Adi Da uses this word with its original Latin meaning of "at the root"—rather than in reference to an extreme (often political) viewpoint.

Reality-art—In his essay "The Maze of Ecstasy", Adi Da summarizes three phases of art history: the pre-Renaissance focus of art on ideas and myths about God (or "God-art"), the post-Renaissance shift to art being an expression of the individual's own "point of view" (or "ego-art"), and his establishment of an art that transcends "point of view" and Reveals Reality Itself ("Reality-art").

Reality Itself / Reality-Condition—Adi Da Samraj distinguishes between two meanings of the word "reality". (1) He refers to reality as we ordinarily perceive it and participate in it as "conditionally manifested reality" (or "conditionality"). This "ordinary reality" is the complex effect of all kinds of causes. Thus, the "ordinary reality" can manifest only in accordance with whatever conditions are the case. Therefore, because the "ordinary reality" is dependent on conditions, Adi Da describes it as "conditionality". (2) In contrast to ordinary reality, Adi Da refers to "Reality Itself" (with capital letters). Reality Itself is not, in any sense, dependent on conditions. In other words, Reality Itself is utterly "Non-conditional". Adi Da states that Reality Itself is the "One and Only Self-Nature, Self-Condition, and Self-State" of every thing and every being in the universe.

"Room"—*See* **"First Room"** *and* **Reality Itself / Reality-Condition**.

root-image—A term Adi Da uses to refer to a single visual image that is the source of the process of image-making in one of his suites.

scientific materialism—The predominant philosophy and worldview of modern humanity, the basic presumption of which is that the material world is all that exists. In scientific materialism, the method of science—the observation of "objective" phenomena—is made into a philosophy and a way of life that suppress the native human impulse to Realize Reality Itself.

"self"—Adi Da places this term in quotation marks to indicate that the presumption of a separate self is an illusion, generated in response to the fact of bodily existence. When the word "self" is used in a reflexive manner (such as in the phrase "self-organizing", meaning "organizing itself"), Adi Da does not use quotation marks.

Self-Consciousness of Reality Itself—In Adi Da's usage, "Self-Consciousness" (with capital "S" and capital "C") does not bear the conventional meaning of embarrassed self-attention, but, rather, indicates the Inherent and Perfect Awareness that is the Fundamental Nature of Reality Itself.

"self"-contraction—Adi Da's descriptive phrase for the ego as the activity of assuming a separate "point of view".

Self-Nature, Self-Condition, and Self-State of Reality Itself—The True "Self" (or "Identity") of Reality Itself—and (thus) the True "Self" (or "Identity") of everything that appears (or what Avatar Adi Da refers to as "all-and-All"). Implicit in Adi Da's use of this phrase is his communication that the Nature of Reality is Transcendental, the Condition of Reality is Spiritual, and (thus) the State of Reality is Conscious Light (or the Indivisibility of the Transcendental Principle of Consciousness and the Spiritual Principle of Energy).

Self-Presentation of Reality Itself—In contrast to "representation" (which involves something standing in for another thing or concept), the Self-Presentation of Reality Itself is Reality's own communication of Itself.

Self-Realization—In the term "Self-Realization", capitalized "Self" refers to Reality Itself—not to a great individual being. Thus, "Self-Realization" is synonymous with "Reality-Realization".

"self"-understanding—Adi Da uses this term to indicate the understanding that the apparent "self" is the activity of contraction.

space-time-"located" / "location" / "locatedness"—*See* **"locatedness" / "location" / "self-locatedness" / space-time-"locatedness"**.

"subject" / "subjective" / non-"subjective"—Adi Da places the lowercase words "subject", "subjective", and so forth, in quotation marks. He does this in order to indicate that, in Reality Itself, there is no such thing as a "subject" that is separate from all potential "objects".

Therefore, when Adi Da describes his art as "non-'subjective'", he is not saying that his images are devoid of a "subjective" (or "inner", or "subtle") dimension, as opposed to an "objective" (or "outer", or physical) dimension. Rather, by referring to his art as "non-'subjective'", he is indicating that his intention is to create art that is not generated on the basis of the artist presuming to be a separate "subject" relating to separate "objects" or presuming the "subject" of the image to be separate from any thing or any one at all.

subtle—*See* **gross, subtle, causal**.

Tacit Intrinsic Self-Apperception / Tacit Intrinsic Self-Apprehension—Inherent and wordless Intuition (of the True Condition, or Reality Itself).

Tacit Self-Recognition—Inherent and wordless "comprehension" (of the True Nature of Reality Itself).

Transcendental—Adi Da Samraj uses the word "Transcendental" with the specific meaning of "transcending (or being beyond) all appearances and experiences".

Transcendental egoless Self-Identity—The True Self of all apparent individual selves. That True Self-Identity of all beings and things is inherently Transcendental.

Transcendental Realism/Realist—In this phrase, Adi Da Samraj uses the word "Realism" or "Realist" (with a capital "R") in a very particular sense. He is not referring to art in which the subject is depicted in a conventionally realistic manner. Rather, he is referring to art that communicates the coincidence of the conditional subject with Non-conditional (or Transcendental) Reality. ■

CATALOG OF WORKS BY ADI DA SAMRAJ

Adi Da's complete catalog of works includes a very large body of drawings and ink paintings (from as early as 1967), a series of miniature self-portraits in enamel paint (1984–1985), a series of paintings in mixed media (1994), and an extensive body of individual photographs in both black-and-white and color (1961–2000). See *The World As Light: An Introduction to the Art of Adi Da Samraj*, by Mei-Ling Israel (Middletown, CA: Da Plastique, 2007), for a discussion and examples of these bodies of work.

Beginning in August 2000, all of Adi Da's work (both camera-based and digitally-based) was created in suites. These suites (from the years 2000–2008) are listed below. It was during the creation of his digitally-based work (2006–2008) that Adi Da Samraj wrote *Transcendental Realism*. In the essays of *Transcendental Realism*, Adi Da refers in general to his camera-based work and in specific to his digitally-based work. Adi Da's principal themes in *Transcendental Realism* are poetically reflected in many of the titles of his suites. ■

Camera-Based Work (2000–2004)

Black-and-White Suites

August 2000–June 2001

Through the Gate. 53 images.

City Light. 52 images.

Tat Sundaram (This Is That Which Is Beautiful). 139 images.

The First Yosemite Suite. 353 images.

Sisters. 13 images.

Four Women. 59 images.

The Burden of Two. 7 images.

The Cult of Pairs. 27 images.

Two Many. 49 images.

The Seat of The Passions. 31 images.

Mother and Daughter. 45 images.

Brahma, Vishnu, and Forsythe. 16 images.

The Aaarghh Suite. 27 images.

Tripura's Seat. 45 images.

Five Men. 20 images.

The Re-Assertion of Perfume in the Instant of Time (Images in Solo and Duo—A Pair Each). 114 images.

She Overhead (The Small Sequence). 8 images.

Repeatedly New. 26 images.

The Wedding Album. 21 images.

The Virgin Suite (An Inexhaustible Supply of Virgins): To Accompany the Iconic Procession of Mother, Daughter, and Male Other in the Room of Mind. 144 images.

The Mere Event (Of Mir and Daily News). 54 images.

Metrix (The Binary Thaw). 142 images.

The Eternal Vigil of Monumental Art. 38 images.

The Analog of Flora Mata (Two Roses Touched by the First Visible Idea of Reality). 168 images.

The Re-Birth of the Idea of Oranges. 45 images.

21 (Exactly). 36 images.

Fun House (The Spherical Skirt): An Indefinitely Unfolding Procession of Iconic Imagery—for He, She, and the Only Horse In The Wild. 658 images.

Open Water. 104 images.

Love's Point Renewed. 297 images.

Videographic Suites

March–October 2001

The Acrylic Block

Spherical Geometry

Ordinary Buddhas

The Revelation Analog: A Binary Intensification of the Original Idea of the Rose

The Accident of Beauty

Already Silent Without Thinking

The Balloon Theory of Everything: After the Spherical Rose Has Fallen from the Ceiling into the Body's Room of Mind

How She Looks. A Still Video Suite of 2,338 images.

Happenine Flora

"Epic" Suites

July 2001–March 2002

Happenine. 1,497 images. Black-and-white.

Odalisque: The Myth of The Reclining Woman—A Suite of 1,845 Images Regarding the Heart's Illusion of Captivity in the Waiting Room of Body and Mind. Black-and-white.

9 Mary: The Superconductivity of Celibate Women Under the Midnight Sun. 2,313 images. Black-and-white.

She Is Mind: The Iconography of Eve. 2,223 images. Black-and-white and color.

"Underwater" Suites

September 2002–May 2003

Plastic Camera #1. 268 images. Color.

Plastic Camera #2. 770 images. Color.

Quandra Loka Mille Camera I–IV. 4,026 images. Black-and-white.

Quandra Loka Mille Camera V. 1,106 images. Color.

Suites of Complex Image-Configurations

May 2003–February 2004

The Breather. 2,662 image-configurations.

Kaleidoscape: Eleven Visions of Countless Points of View. 6,211 image-configurations.

The Spherical Tower. 3,912 image-configurations.

Three. 2,787 image-configurations.

Images 2004. 8,061 image-configurations.

Digitally-Based Work (2006–2008)

Spectra Suites

April–July 2006

Spectra One: The Pastimes of Narcissus. 103 images.

Spectra Two: A Horse Appears In The Wild Is Always Already The Case. 475 images.

Spectra Three: Quandra Contemplating the Fruits of Perfect Knowledge. 107 images.

Spectra Four: The Room Itself Is The Only Witness To The Three Common States. 189 images.

Spectra Five: Not-Two Is Peace. 48 images.

Spectra Six: Not-Two Is Not Two. 24 images.

Spectra Seven: The Self-Portrait. 24 images.

Spectra Eight: Life Is The Perfect Reflection Of Its Source. 37 images.

Spectra Nine: The Autobiography Of Everybody. 75 images.

Spectra Ten: The "First Room" Trilogy. 126 images.

Perfect Mirror Suites

July–August 2006

The Perfect Mirror One: The Voyage. 87 images.

The Perfect Mirror Two: This Is Not-An-Object. 69 images.

The Perfect Mirror Three: Portrait Of The Artist As Not-An-Object. 11 images.

Geome Suites

August–October 2006

Geome One: Alberti's Window. 1,416 images.

Geome Two: 2001. 1,101 images.

Geome Three: The Scale of Perfection. 5,454 images.

Geome Four: The Subject In Question. 354 images.

Geome Five: Ciqomi (Acception). 833 images.

Oculus Suites

July 2006–May 2007

Oculus One: The Reduction Of The Beloved To Love Alone. 2,644 images.

Oculus Two: Alberti's Room. 160 images.

"Geome and Linead" Suites

May–October 2007

Orpheus One: The Spiritual Descent of The Bicycle Becomes The Second-Birth of Flight. 188 images.

Linead One: Eurydice One—The Illusory Fall of The Bicycle Into The Sub-Atomic Parallel Worlds of Primary Color and Point of View. 37 images.

The Goddess of New York. 633 images.

"Geome, Linead, and Orphic Font" Suites
November 2007–November 2008

The Orphic Font. 27 images.

The Struwwelpeter Suite (The ego-"I" and The Straightener): Contemplating The Mind/Body Problem and The Bodily Illusion Of Being a Separate "self". Total of 2,592 images.

Part One: Gross Boy Peter (The ego-"I"). 361 images.

Part Two: Good Dog Tray and The Cruel Frederick ("self" vs. "not-self"). 152 images.

Part Three: The Self-Illumination Of Harriet (The Insufficiency Of A Merely Mental Enlightenment). 224 images.

Part Four: Saint Nick's Equalizer (The Straightener Is Not-Two). 399 images.

Part Five: The Near-Sighted Huntsman and The Far-Sighted Hare, or, The Hunter-Hero At Your Back Vs. The Edible Rabbit In Your Face (Whereas Mind and Body Is Not-Two). 460 images.

Part Six: Childish Conrad and The Evil Thumb-Tailor, or, The Boogeyman Always Bobs Both (It Is Your Fear What Takes The Life Out Of You, Because The Mind Always Deceives The Body). 209 images.

Part Seven: Helvetica and The Shocking Five-Day Count, or, Life Is Death Or So By Number Soup The Body Thinks (It Is The Mind What Kills The Body, Because The Body Always Deceives The Mind). 787 images.

The World As Light:
An Introduction to the Art of
Adi Da Samraj
by Mei-Ling Israel

A profusely illustrated overview of Adi Da Samraj's entire artistic oeuvre up to early 2007—accompanied by key statements he made on his own art and on the artistic process in general.

Softcover; 128 pages, color and black-and-white illustrations.
$24.95

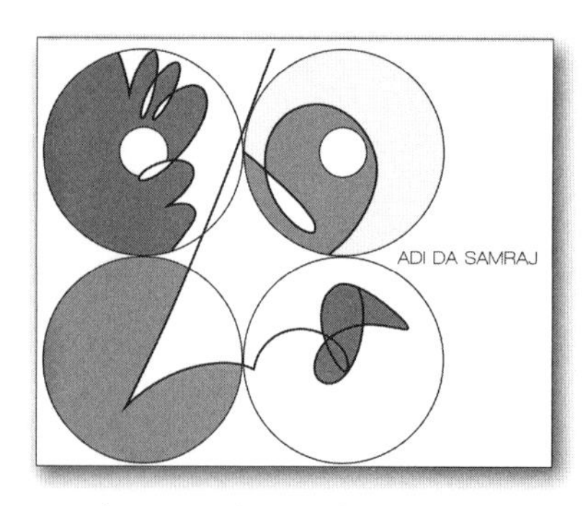

Adi Da Samraj:
Orpheus and Linead
Catalog of solo exhibition
at Sundaram Tagore Gallery,
New York City, 2010
With essay by curator
Achille Bonito Oliva

Adi Da's startlingly modern images of the ancient mythical archetypes of Orpheus and Eurydice, portrayed both through unexpected juxtapositions of everyday figures and objects and through entirely abstract figuration. These works—combining digitally modified photographic imagery with hand-drawn elements and digitally generated forms—portray, in an "abstract narrative", an Orpheus who "never looks back".

The catalog reproduces the eleven monumental pieces in the exhibition, together with other works from Adi Da's suites *Orpheus One* and *Linead One.*

Softcover; 48 pages, full-color images.
$29.95

The Spectra Suites

by Adi Da Samraj

In the ten *Spectra* suites, Adi Da Samraj combines digital and camera-based work to create a series of dynamic and vibrantly colored visual worlds.

Adi Da Samraj's Spectra Suites *flood and suffuse the body and mind of the perceiver in colors and forms, affording pure joy. But they are carefully equilibrated in a narrative structure, conveying a sense of equanimity and balance as well as "supersensual delight".*

—Donald Kuspit,
Distinguished art critic

The Spectra Suites is the first major full-color monograph on Adi Da's art, published by Welcome Books in conjunction with the collateral exhibition of his work at the 2007 Venice Biennale.

Hardcover; 140 pages, full-color images with seven gatefolds.
$95.00

Transcendental Realism: The Art of Adi Da Samraj

Catalog of collateral exhibition at the 2007 Venice Biennale

With essays by curators Achille Bonito Oliva and Peter Frank, and an Artist's Statement by Adi Da Samraj

Monumental works from Adi Da's *Spectra*, *Geome*, and *Oculus* suites are reproduced in stunning color.

Adi Da Samraj's two- and three-dimensional shapes are always concrete communicative realities, statements of a mental order that is never repressive or closed off, but always germinating and unpredictable. In all instances, shapes germinate and multiply with sudden offshoots that reveal the potential of a new geometric eroticism.

—Achille Bonito Oliva
Distinguished art critic, past Director of the Venice Biennale

Softcover; 50 pages, color and black-and-white images with one gatefold.
$29.95

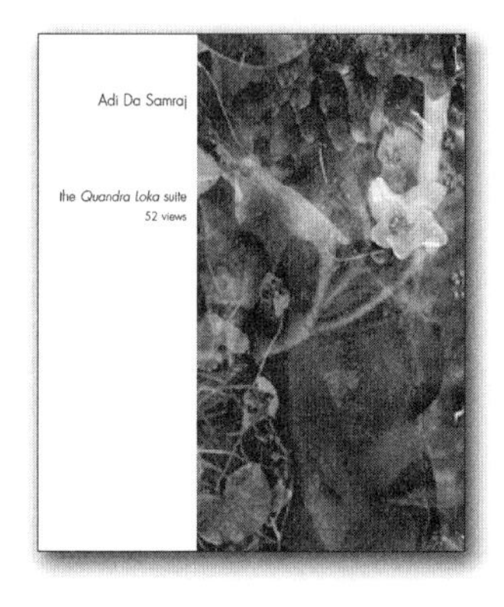

The *Quandra Loka* Suite: 52 Views

Catalog of solo exhibition at Louis Stern Fine Arts, Los Angeles, 2003

This large-format catalog pictures a series of fifty-two works from the *Quandra Loka* suite.

It is a rare artist who can convey, convincingly, the sense of being face to face with the source of being. Adi Da can clearly live in the depths without succumbing to their pressure, bringing back pearls of art to prove it.

—from the introduction by Donald Kuspit

Softcover; 128 pages, sepia-tone images.
$49.95

The Bright Field

Black-and-white photographic images from 2000–2001

This first publication of Adi Da's art features selected images from twelve suites, each different in quality: a "meditation" on a rock that rises out the of the ocean, a series of sensual and playful images set in a city, a look at human personalities as "shattered" phenomena, and so on.

Most of Adi Da's images in this book are complex and sophisticated multiple exposures, often involving more than two (and even as many as ten or more) superimposed layers, shot in camera.

Softcover; 88 pages, duo-tone images.
$34.95

To order these and other books, tapes, CDs, DVDs, and videos by and about Adi Da Samraj, contact

THE DAWN HORSE PRESS

1-877-770-0772 (from within North America)

1-707-928-6653 (from outside North America)

Or visit the Dawn Horse Press website: **www.dawnhorsepress.com**

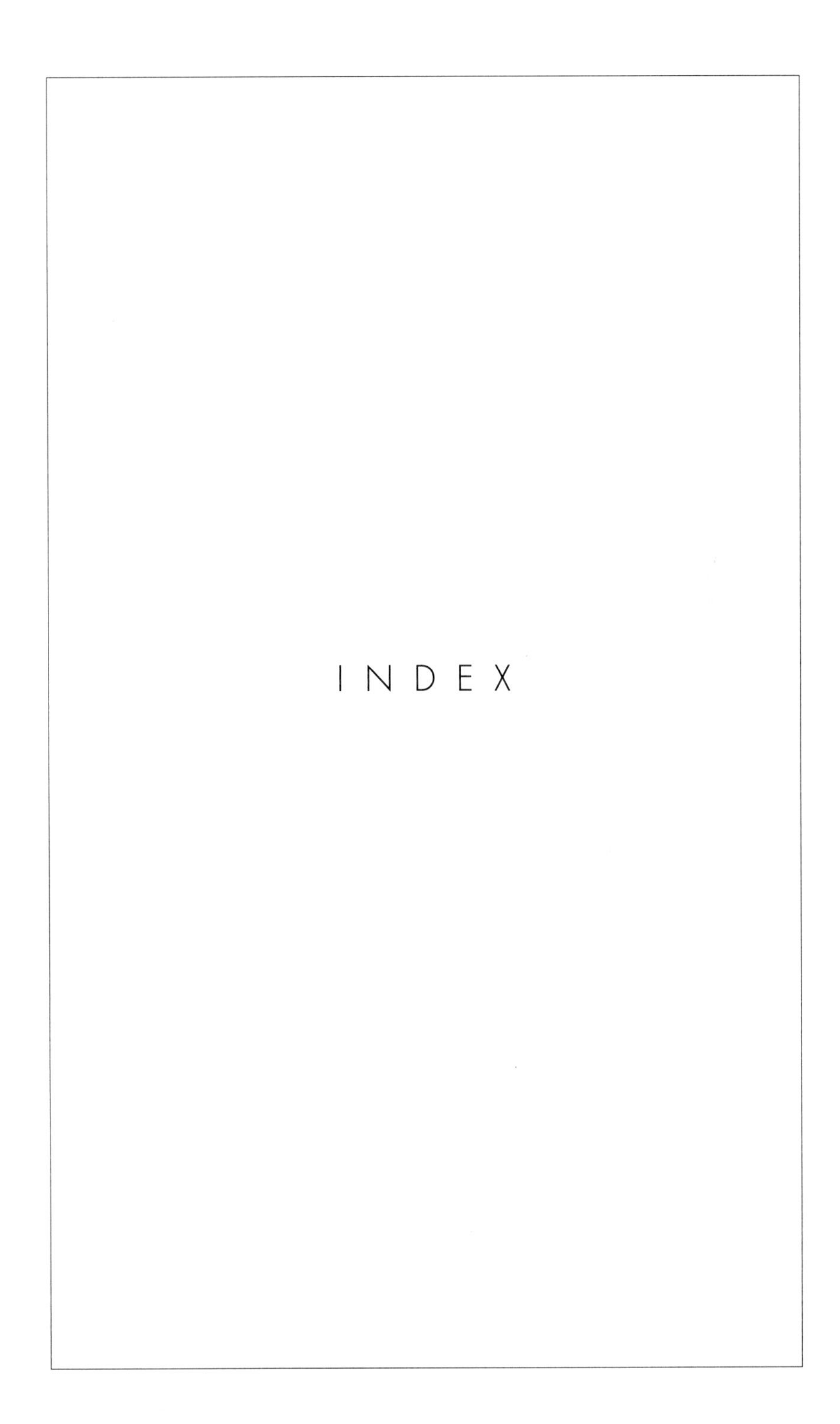

INDEX

INDEX

Note to the reader: Page numbers in *italic* type indicate references in the front and back matter. All other page numbers refer to the main body of the text. Definitions of terms can be found in the glossary, pp. 237–42.